YOU CANNOT CAGE THE WOLF

You Cannot Cage *the Wolf*

a mother struggles with the suicide of her soldier son

Cynthia Crosson

Haley's

Athol,

Massachusetts

Haley's • 488 South Main Street • Athol, MA 01331
haley.antique@verizon.net • 978.249.9400

Copy edited by Debra Ellis. Cover image from Shutterstock.

Lyrics from "The Dance," page 33, by Tony Arata as recorded by Garth Brooks on the 1990 album, *Garth Brooks,* 44629, released by Capitol Nashville.

Lyrics from "Three Wooden Crosses," pages 36 and 136, by Kim Edwin Williams and Douglas M. Johnson, as recorded by Randy Travis on the 2002 single, *Rise and Shine,* released by Curb Music.

Passage, pages 39 and 127, from *Animal Speak: The Spiritual and Magical Powers of Creatures Great and Small* by Ted Williams, Llewellyn Publications, St. Paul, 2004.

Lyrics from "Here I Am, Lord," page 81, by Dan Schutte, published by Oregon Catholic Press, 1981.

Library of Congress Cataloging-in-Publication Data

Names: Crosson-Tower, Cynthia, author.

Title: You cannot cage the wolf : a mother struggles with the suicide of

her soldier son / Cynthia Crosson.

Other titles: Mother struggles with the suicide of her soldier son

Description: Athol, Massachusetts : Haley's, [2020] | Summary:

"Psychotherapist and Christian minister Cynthia Crosson reviews events

leading to the suicide of her young adult son, Jamie, after his return

from service with the US Army in Bosnia. She reflects on how she missed

signs that he experienced post-traumatic stress disorder, PTSD. The

author finds solace as she develops programs involving service dogs for

veterans"-- Provided by publisher.

Identifiers: LCCN 2019041821 | ISBN 9781948380171 (paperback) | ISBN 978-1-948380-21-8 (hardback) | ISBN 978-1-948380-22-5 (ebook: ePub)

Subjects: LCSH: Crosson-Tower, Cynthia. | Veterans--Suicidal

behavior--United States. | Mothers of soldiers--United

States--Biography. | Mothers of suicide victims--United

States--Biography. | Post-traumatic stress disorder--Patients--United

States. | Tower, James Crosson, 1980-2003. | Yugoslav War,

1991-1995--Veterans--United States--Biography. | Suicide victims--United

States--Biography. | Psychiatric service dogs--United States.

Classification: LCC HV6545.7 .C76 2020 | DDC 362.28/3092 [B]--dc23

LC record available at https://lccn.loc.gov/2019041821

in memory of Jamie, child of my heart

and

for all loved ones of soldiers and veterans who have lost hope
may reading our story give you hope for healing

There is no greater agony than

bearing an untold story inside you.

—Maya Angelou

James Crosson Tower

1980-2003

James Crosson Tower and his mom, Cynthia Crosson

Contents

Something Good from Something that Has No Good

a foreword by Beverly Prestwood-Taylor, DMin

"If something good can come from something that has no good in it, then what is there that cannot be accomplished?" wrote Jamie, child of author Cynthia Crosson's heart, in a letter home from his deployment to Bosnia. He refers to a young Bosnian woman raped as the spoils of war but paradoxically filled with hope from the child born to her out of an act of despicable violence.

Cynthia's narrative of the stunning news of Jamie's death by suicide fifteen years ago and the spiritual and emotional growth she discovers in the journey of healing testify to the truth of her son's prescient words. Multiple good emerges from the way Cynthia navigates her healing journey.

Her willingness to tell her story in *You Cannot Cage the Wolf* further testifies to her growth. She reveals vulnerability. Beginning with anguish and denial, then finding courage to acknowledge shame and regret, she records her progress. Eventually, she finds a way to celebrate a life lived and knowledge that her relationship with her son continues to grow.

You Cannot Cage the Wolf validates experiences of families whose precious children die by suicide after returning from deployment.

Even though an expert in the study of post-traumatic stress syndrome, PTSD, Cynthia did not recognize the import of her son's disorder. Starkly honest about her failure to recognize his private pain and about her extreme depression after his death, she doesn't minimize the long, arduous process of healing. A trained therapist and ordained pastor, she confesses to moments when she had no answers.

Twenty-two service members die by suicide every day. A federal department of defense update shows an alarming uptick in suicides of women and men between the ages of eighteen and twenty-four in spite of concerted official effort to address the situation. Families left behind must muddle through the fog of unfathomable challenge of surviving the devastation as they struggle to get through each day during the first years and eventually, to live again.

There is no easy path to recovery, no rules to follow nor steps to take that make sense to mothers, fathers, sisters, brothers, and loved ones. Those left behind must figure out how to keep going. Cynthia's narrative demonstrates a way to focus on the smallest details, as she describes the beaded choker her son wore or the white, sand-like ashes that remained of the body she once cradled.

As she offers a vivid account of her daily life, we can walk with her, find awe in a field of buttercups, and see deeper meaning in mundane events, like the feathers that mystically appear when she thought of her son.

She shows how to look for and see signposts that can lead mourners along a winding path toward transcendence.

Cynthia's healing continued as she fought her depression by doing good based on the skills and gifts she had. And she saw many signs along the way to point her in a new direction. She studied for ordination as a pastor. She adopted a service dog for ministry, a commitment that led her to help develop a program that provides service dogs for veterans with PTSD. She remains dedicated to working with veterans and service dogs.

Readers of *You Cannot Cage the Wolf* will discover descriptions of PTSD and will learn about the symptoms of PTSD suffered by combat veterans. They will also be able to identify their own symptoms of trauma, called secondary PTSD, caused by the shock of the news of their family members death. In identifying and naming the secondary trauma families live with, they also find more ways to heal.

Antonio Machado, a nineteenth-century Spanish poet says, "There is no path. We make the path by walking." Each one of us has to walk our own, distinctive path, sometimes for healing. In walking her path, Cynthia has gained the strength to share wisdom hard-earned.

"What if? What if?"

a prologue by Cynthia Crosson

The young man strides confidently across the stage, each step a tribute to how far this former Marine has come. The dog at his side looks expectantly up at him. As he reaches out for his diploma with one hand, the young man strokes the dog's soft ears with the other. Applause rises from the packed auditorium of onlookers. Knowing I had helped make this moment possible for him, I look on with tears of pride.

My own small service dog, curled at my feet, rises and leans against me, gazing up as he does when he senses my sadness or upset. His soft brown eyes speak comfort as no human can. Does he imagine grief causes my tears? Perhaps he is more perceptive than I thought. Residual grief may mingle with my gratification in the achievement of the young veteran. I reach down and stroke the dog's fuzzy grey head, smiling and silently assuring him that I am fine. But even as I do, words echo in my head, "What if? What if?"

The room quiets as the veteran begins to speak.

"This dog has saved my life." He pauses, obviously trying to maintain control. "After I returned from Iraq, I was a different person. My body may not have been injured, but my mind definitely as. I came close to losing my wife and my children until I learned of this program. And now I have my dog, and with him, I also got my family back. Thank you." Clearly, that emotion overwhelms him so that he can no longer continue. He retreats from the stage into the arms of his family, and the crowd renews its applause.

I am among the audience at the semi-annual graduation of NEADS, an agency that places trained service dogs with people with disabilities. And this veteran whom I had helped get his dog is not the only one whose life has been saved. I remember him well from when he first applied for a service dog. He was unable to leave his home, so fearful was he of being attacked. Instead, mired in depression, he isolated himself while he grew more and more distant from his family and friends. Hearing that many of his brothers and sisters in arms had committed suicide did not help his depression. I know that, more than once, this soldier too had considered taking his own life. But placing a service dog with him had given him new purpose, eased his anxiety, and helped him to go out in crowds with confidence that he had a "battle buddy" beside him.

Service dogs like his had helped bring meaning to my life, too. As I listen to him and watch him interact with his dog, I see my own son Jamie in his face. A thought crosses my mind again as it has so many times since I began to witness the healing brought to veterans through their dogs: "If only Jamie could be standing there."

I dab my eyes as I watch the next of my veterans, his dog at his side, mount the stage to receive his diploma. My pride in the young man mingles with the remembered pain of Jamie's death. Why couldn't Jamie have found a renewed purpose for his life as this veteran had? Why didn't I see the pain Jamie experienced before it was too late? After all I am a psychiatric social worker, psychotherapist, and emerita college professor who prepared students to become therapists who themselves would someday treat troubled minds and hearts after the ravages that facing combat could leave. In retirement, I forged a new career from a long ago-dream of being a minister.

As I watch yet another young veteran and his dog leave the stage and emerge into the crowd and the expectant and proud embrace of his wife and family, a feeling of warmth overtakes me. "I'll be okay," I whisper to myself. "I'm really okay now."

It was almost as though I can hear Jamie's voice and feel his strong warm arms around me. The faint breeze from ceiling fans seems to echo his words. "I know you are, Mom. And I'm proud of *you!*"

I was not always sure I would find the peace I have this day. It had been years of pain and struggle to extricate myself from the quicksand of depression and grief. I am lucky, in spite of everything. I had the love of my two other sons, Chay and Andrew, and of my husband, Jim. Even my sons' father, my former husband, Charlie, had been there for me.

It wasn't easy for any of them, either. Grief wracked them, too, and there were times when they, too, wondered if I would ever be myself again. But even as we heal, do we ever return to the place we were before the world shattered around us?

The death of my son Jamie shattered my world and my family's world, too. Shattering, too, was the cruel irony of my mother's death just weeks later. And yet, somehow I emerged—partially because, over time, I confronted the truth and internalized it, vowing to carry on with the help of not only my loving family but also the unconditional love of a little dog—the catalyst—that gave me a new focus. Through the experience, I gained impetus to find meaning in my son's death as I developed a program to help veterans wounded by combat in mind and body to find their own solace in a service dog.

ad learned plenty about myself and my resilience. I emerged stronger and more in tune with who I am than ever before.

Healing was not easy. Yet, in great pain, we learn to know our strength. I remember in vivid Technicolor each painful step toward finding that strength.

Shattering Glass

"Your son is dead," announces the beefy police chief at my door that Sunday, May 18, 2003. No preamble. To the point. And with those words, the Chief and I freeze in memory's tableau. I can feel my life shatter like glass, cracks moving outward until in slow motion they agonizingly separate and fall one by one hitting the floor with sounds that tell you that the deed is done and cannot be reversed.

"No!" The agonized cry seems not to come from me but rather from somewhere in the depths of my soul. And I sob deep sobs that I could no more control than I can the event that had caused them.

Later I would wonder why I had not questioned the chief's pronouncement. Why had I not doubted or assumed that someone had made a terrible mistake and that my twenty-two-year-old son Jamie would walk through the door with his cheery, "Hi, Ma!" and life would go on as it should? Jamie, the child of my heart—his oversized smile even now, in memory, lights up our lives. That I would no longer see that smile in actuality was incomprehensible. And yet, on that Sunday morning I never question the truth in the chief's statement, even though the reality has not fully hit me that Jamie is gone.

My mother, my comforter since childhood, reaches for me, but at that moment I cannot be held. For being held would admit to the possibility of comfort, and there was nothing that can ease the pain or rework the splinters of shattered glass into a whole again. Unable to console me, she asks the logical question that I could not form, "What happened?"

As I hear her voice, I gaze at her. Tears have already streaked her agonized face. In that moment I realize that she, too, has lost Jamie—her beloved grandchild. We are united in our pain.

"We believe that he shot himself," comes the answer. Shot himself? Not Jamie. Not my son, so full of life.

"Can I call someone for you?" The chief is still there, now more subdued and seeking to soften the blow he has been compelled by his job to administer.

"My husband," I murmur weakly. On some level, I know it won't be easy to get my husband, who is out of phone range. The chief knows Jim and knows that, as a mill owner, Jim will be at the sawmill where there is no phone. The chief nods and leaves the house, ostensibly to find my husband.

The messenger who brought the news that would change my life has left. I begin to grapple with the reality that my son is dead, although the truth of it has not set in and won't fully do so for some time. Quickly, I dial my pastor—another person who will bring comfort. It is a Sunday. My mom and I have just come from church. We are both very fond of Reverend Lois Buchiane. Probably herself just having returned home from church, she answers quickly.

"Jamie shot himself," I hear myself say.

"I'll be right there." She says without hesitation.

I know the other call I must make. It is to Jamie's father from whom I had been divorced for more than five years. Despite a rather difficult divorce, Charlie and I have forged an amicable relationship for the sake of our children. Later I don't even remember his response when I gave him the news, but I know that he was as bereft as I was. He, too, is soon at the house.

Mechanically, I call those who need to be called, especially my oldest son, Chay, at graduate school in California, the other side of the country from our Massachusetts home. Not speaking at first, he is stunned. There is a catch in his voice when he finally responds. "What should I do, Mom?"

"I don't know. I don't know what *I* am doing," I breathe. "I'll call you when I know more."

I know that my youngest son should also be told, but at that moment, the effort is beyond me.

"We need to tell Andrew." It may have been Charlie who pronounced those necessary words. And surely it is Charlie who asks, "Would you like me to go up to tell him?"

Andrew, our fourteen-year-old, lives in a residential treatment center a few towns away. Life has not been easy for our youngest son diagnosed with a variety of conditions including attention deficit disorder with hyperactivity or ADHD, anxiety disorder, and learning disabilities, all of which made him different from others. Asperger's syndrome, a form of high functioning autism, would come to be the most accurate diagnosis.

Whatever the nomenclature of his diagnosis, Andrew's brother has died, and the information will hit him hard. More assured in delivering bad news than I, his father would be the ideal person to deliver the sad news to Andrew. I also know that, for Andrew's sake, I should be there, too. When I finally accept that we were not living an unbelievable nightmare—that Jamie's death is real—Charlie and I will go together to tell Andrew.

The next few hours blur by. Little did we know it is our time of respite. Later in the day, we will be called upon to face the details of iie's death as the police interrogate us. But before the interrogation, at home with those who loved him, we have time to remember the good things. I know Jim, Charlie, my mother, and I talked about Jamie and special little things we treasured about him. He was such a charmer. I don't remember much about that day. There was only the terrible, growing ache at the loss of the child of my heart.

Jamie was our middle child between Chay, our very bright oldest who distinguished himself academically, as an actor and musician, and in so many other ways, and Andrew, loving and talented in his own way but whose special needs require a great deal of our attention.

Years before, I remember having one of those cuddly times that moms have with their children as I put a much younger Jamie to bed. Perhaps seven years old, Jamie seemed particularly clingy, and I knew there was something on his mind. That week Chay was deeply involved in some activity—perhaps a play, and we had experienced a tough time with Andrew's medical problems.

I soon realized that Jamie wondered about his own place in our family of complex relationships. I knew that Jamie, undoubtedly still Mommy's boy, needed me. So I talked with him about how special he was and how much we loved him. I told him about his unique and essential place in my heart. He brightened. "So I'm the child of your heart?" he asked.

Ever after he referred to himself as the child of my heart—not to disparage the other two boys but rather assuring himself of his place in my affections. In fact, his letters written throughout his time in the military were always signed, "Child of Your Heart."

To allow one child to call himself the child of my heart when we had two other children may seem preferential, but I know—as hopefully they do as well—that all my children mean the world to me. I always refer to Jamie as the child of my heart. His death truncated our relationship. I have the rest of my life to demonstrate to my sons Chay and Andrew how much I love them.

My oldest, Chay, distinguished himself from the very beginning of his life. Everybody's darling for his cheerful, winning personality, he enjoyed four years of undivided attention before Jamie's birth. After a brief period of jealousy when a new sibling ousted him from his position as "only," Chay adjusted well. He excelled not only in studies but in music and theatre. After finding his voice in a musical revue, Chay quickly won the role of Kurt, the youngest boy in *The Sound of Music,* at our local community theatre. Other roles followed, and he would later develop his musical talent by playing piano and organ.

And Andrew was born with many health challenges that necessitated constant vigilance and worry. Despite it all, he remained undaunted and with more spirit to survive than most people. Of course, we love him dearly. All of our children are, even now, integral parts of my heart, but only Jamie so identified. His death tore out a piece of my own heart and left a hole that would never fully heal.

Sensational headlines resulted from the events surrounding his death and brought the media to my door, robbing us of the privacy to grieve in peace. Family and friends lovingly conspired to shield me from lurid media reports, and it was years later before I read them. They said that Jamie had broken into the police station in our small town, stolen weapons, and invaded the home in a nearby town where Jamie's former girlfriend slept with her new man. There had been a tussle. Jamie had killed himself.

For years (and sometimes even now), I could not believe that the reports had any validity or merit. Not my Jamie. More than ten years later, reviewing the autopsy report with a friend, I came to the nearly inescapable conclusion that it would have been virtually impossible for anyone else to have inflicted the wound that killed my son.

While the police and other officials may have alluded to the facts and innuendo spewed by the press in the days immediately following Jamie's death, I did not really take in more than the fact that the child of my heart would never again in this life hug me or laugh with me or be here at all.

I do not remember how we first learned details of the events surrounding Jamie's death. They were so out of sync with the son I knew. But how could he have been the same person I had tearfully seen off to Army basic training five years earlier? How could he have been? If someone goes to college for five years, is he the same? If someone moves away for five years, is he the same?

I remember well how his letters changed over the course of his enlistment. He filled his first letters, from basic training, with optimism and enthusiasm as well as accounts of fatigue.

Initially, he took to Army life. In high school, Jamie had spent all four years on the football team, and I believe that Army camaraderie mimicked the football experience for him. He was popular with other boys on his high school team and played the game well. His grandmother could not understand why he enjoyed playing a game that constantly "ended up in pig piles," her way of describing tackles.

Jamie patiently explained that the experience was not as much the game as it was team cooperation. "Being part of a bunch of guys training and working for the same goal is inspiring," he told her.

We, his family—including my mother—went to every game during his senior year when the team won the high school Super Bowl.

Knowing that Jamie often heard his father and stepfather revel in stories about the buddies they made in the military, I should not have been surprised when Jamie chose a life he hoped would offer him similar camaraderie. I knew, too, that Jamie felt strongly about our country and would see military service as a worthwhile commitment to our country. Jamie, the eternal rescuer, once told me that he felt that being a soldier was a way of protecting a country that he loved—something he could do that not everyone could.

Filled with optimism and anxious to assume his role as a soldier, Jamie left for basic training at Fort Benning, Georgia, in August of 1998. He had enlisted for an eight-year stretch with high hopes of being an airborne United States Army Ranger, but even though he passed the qualifying exam, the Army assigned him to the mechanized infantry. Jamie appeared to take it in his stride, although I could feel his disappointment. I wondered why he did not appeal, as he had his heart set on the prestigious assignment. After he passed the exam, I could not believe that he accepted the different assignment, although knowing the military, he no doubt knew he had no choice. Nonetheless, he was anxious to begin his military career and enthusiastically assumed the job assigned him. Jamie would come to enjoy the mechanized infantry unit that became his military role.

His letters during basic training told me he had found the camaraderie that he craved. He had many buddies. As he related his escapades, he wrote to me with humor of their trials and adventures. For example, as a training exercise, their drill sergeant ordered Jamie and his group of trainees to dig foxholes, ostensibly for practice. After dark, the sergeant ordered the trainees into the foxholes for another exercise.

Jamie's teammate descended into their foxhole with Jamie close behind. With a startled yelp, the fellow soldier scrambled hastily out of the foxhole, Jamie at his heels. Excitedly, they explained there was something down there, moving and cold and armored. They wondered if it was some military booby trap designed for their training. Armed with flashlights, the two trainees boldly faced the threat and discovered that, during their dinner, a hapless armadillo had fallen into the hole and could not get out.

I never learned the fate of the poor armadillo but believe that if ,....ie was part of the decision, the animal went safely on its way. Jamie always loved animals no matter what the kind.

He filled his letters from military life with tales of his team, squad, and platoon members, many of whom became his buddies—people who trained and later worked with him. He had never been afraid of hard work and seemed undaunted by the rigorous Army life. Each part of training became a new challenge for Jamie, one he took on with relish. He soon wrote home to tell that he had qualified as an expert marksman, quite a feat for a young man whose prior experience with firearms was a course on the BB gun at Boy Scout camp.

At Thanksgiving the year of Jamie's boot camp, my soon-to-be husband, Jim; Charlie, Jamie's dad; Andrew, my mom, and I drove to Georgia to witness Jamie' s graduation from basic training. Having Thanksgiving dinner in an Army mess hall provided a new experience, and much to my surprise, the meal was delicious. The Army did a laudable job of catering the event. More than compensating for not being at home, I shared his special time of achievement with the child of my heart.

Even more impressive than the Thanksgiving meal was Jamie's graduation from basic training. The day before graduation, Jamie and his fellow trainees each received blue cords for their dress uniforms designating their places in the infantry.

Graduation day dawned chilly but fair. We sat on cold metal bleachers as soldiers demonstrated a mock battle ended by the "good guys" in tanks rolling on the field to claim their victory. And then in the distance we saw a parade of hundreds of uniformed men and women in Class A uniforms marching in perfect precision in companies that came ever closer. These were the graduates—our graduates—and we could not have been more proud.

We had a brief opportunity to congratulate them after the ceremony. Jamie beamed in his new role. Proud, happy, and convinced that Jamie had found his niche in military life, we left Fort Benning.

After basic training, the Army stationed Jamie at Fort Riley in Kansas where he found a new group of buddies. He seemed content with his life in the Army and made friends who supported and cared for him for the rest of his life.

We savored his letters telling us mostly of his activities with his buddies. Before the days when soldiers regularly used email to keep in touch with loved ones, letters sustained us. Jamie rose in rank from private to specialist. He trained in mechanized infantry in preparation for his eventual assignment to a Bradley Fighting Vehicle, an armored transport that provides cover as soldiers engage in warfare. I looked up pictures of the Bradley and felt more confident that Jamie would be safe in one of those huge tanks.

After a brief leave when Jamie and his brothers gave me away to Jim at our wedding, Jamie received orders to duty in war-torn Bosnia. A peacekeeping mission, they called it. He deployed, as the official language puts it, and we began to receive Jamie's letters from his duty post. We realized that his life in Bosnia was hardly peaceful. Soldiers had little opportunity to go out without concern for their safety, as land mines planted by warring factions dotted the area outside the Army post and improvised explosive devises, IEDs, were a constant threat.

I can only imagine what faced the young men and women sent to Bosnia in the aftermath of the war. US soldiers often found themselves in the middle of frequent violent clashes between Serbs and Muslims. The soldiers' mandate to diffuse and deescalate violence sometimes resulted in anger and aggression turned on them.

It fell to Jamie's squad to provide a security detail as local nationals exhumed the long dead from mass graves. After ascertaining that individuals might or might not be identified, the remains

̣ reburied more respectfully in individual graves. "It was
̤.......ɔst more difficult to watch," one of Jamie's teammates later told
me, "than to do the actual digging. It got to a lot of the guys." My
heart ached to imagine my caring, sensitive nineteen-year-old son
required to be a part of such a task.

Their time in Bosnia affected many of the young soldiers despite
not necessarily being in active combat. The uncertainty of never
knowing who or what might prove a threat meant that even in their
down time, the soldiers felt the need to be on guard. What got to
Jamie the most was the stark contrast between how people lived
in the US and how they lived in the war zone. "They literally have
nothing," he remarked to one of his buddies, "and yet, the kids are
still smiling."

Nevertheless, beauty also shone in letters that Jamie sent home.
I took inspiration from his efforts to find meaning in all that he
experienced.

Jamie wrote of his time in Bosnia:

> None of it makes any sense. There are no good guys and
> no bad guys. The newspapers make such a big deal out of the
> Serbs killing the Muslims but neglect to say that the Muslims
> have no qualms about killing the Serbs, either. Is it really
> worth killing someone simply because they are of a different
> religion or have different values? How could anyone look into
> the innocent eyes of the Bosnian children and see anything
> but the reflection of how wrong this fighting is? It would be
> enough to lose hope unless you bear witness to the fact that,
> regardless of the sometimes heinous and destructive nature of
> man, life does triumph.

Among Jamie's photos was one of him on a well-known bridge
surrounded by Bosnian children. Jamie loved children and I was not
at all surprised that he would attract them even in a war-torn country.

Jamie spoke, too, of how a young woman who had been raped
as part of ethnic cleansing nonetheless found comfort in the child
that resulted—a child that many of her contemporaries would have

aborted or killed at birth in response to how it was conceived. But this young woman was different and Jamie admired her ability to persevere in the face of evil. In his letter, he wrote:

> Regardless of all that had happened to her, she says that she could never be happier, thanks to the child born of evil men. The irony is rather sad, really. At the same time, it gives so much hope. If something good can come from something that has no good in it, then what is there that cannot be accomplished? I only hope that there are other ways to bring about good than as a result of evil. One thing I know is that if I ever feel sorry for myself, I can look back on how the people of Bosnia have shown their strength and fortitude in the face of problems greater than anything I will ever face.

Despite his earnest philosophizing, his experiences took a toll on Jamie. I can't believe I didn't recognize the obvious. When he returned on leave, he was a different young man than the boy who had optimistically pledged himself to Army life. Often separating himself to write in his journal or read, he was quiet and contemplative. He told us that he no longer enjoyed the frivolous party lives of his local contemporaries, his former football buddies.

He angered quickly and slumped into depression. Unexpected noises startled him, and he reacted defensively. Sleep eluded him, and I was awakened by noises in the night only to encounter Jamie unable to sleep and prowling the house in the wee hours. As a therapist, I may have realized that Jamie endured the post-traumatic stress (PTSD) we see in so many soldiers today. But as a mother, blinded by my desire to ease my son's obvious pain, I did not seek a diagnosis but rather longed to hold and comfort him so that the pain would go away.

I was not alone in my failure to recognize my son's emotional and psychological condition. At that time, PTSD was not the common diagnosis it is among veterans from Iraq and Afghanistan. Those returning from Vietnam often showed signs of PTSD, and many resent the fact that it was never addressed until years had

by. Every war has seen the symptoms—from the American civil
.... where the condition was known as "soldier's heart" to later
reports of "shell shock" or "battle fatigue." Only after Vietnam was
it called post-traumatic stress disorder while still often being hidden
in shame by its victims. Veterans did not want to admit to PTSD
lest they appear weak in the eyes of others. Jamie would never have
admitted to having such a problem. It was not the macho thing to
do. Fortunately, the psychological community and the public now
recognize, give a name to, and provide treatment for the condition
once hidden in plain sight. But when Jamie came home from Bosnia,
PTSD was a shameful diagnosis.

I have heard some say that Bosnia in the late 1990s and early
2000s was not really a combat zone, but violence was still very
much present. I knew from my work with trauma survivors that the
unpredictability and the expectation of violence can give rise to
trauma. And the fact that the military personnel never knew when
the next mine would explode, the next shot be fired, or the next
assault come certainly served to create anxiety. It is not surprising
that a so-called peacekeeping mission could lead to trauma among
many of those stationed there.

Did the emotional wounds of war cause my caring young son,
who loved people and life, to choose to leave this world when his
life had barely begun to unfold?

Through the Shards

Over the next few days, we await the return of our son's body from the state medical examiner. I try not to think what an autopsy meant in terms of cutting up the body I had birthed and loved so well. Dwelling on that creates an almost visceral pain. Instead, I try to focus on how we will say goodbye to him at his memorial service.

Aching with the memories that accompanied pictures, I comb through old photographs, my fingers sometimes caressing the shiny images that depict my son who was. There was infant Jamie already blessed with a crop of black hair that—if we believe old wives' tales—gave me the great deal of heartburn I experienced as I carried him under my heart.

He revealed his enthusiasm for life in his very first moments on earth. He began as—and ever was—someone who loved to eat. In fact, when he grew older, his father and I embarrassed him by calling him the baby barracuda to describe how vigorously he nursed. In his adolescent years, a gallon of orange juice disappeared in a day.

I come upon several albums of the early years of Jamie's life and let them take me back for a moment of peaceful remembrance.

When I learned that I was pregnant with Jamie, I worried that I did not have enough love for a second child. That might sound strange to people with siblings or several children, but as an only child, I had basked in my parents' adoration for all of my childhood. Despite wishing sometimes that I had a brother or sister, I was secretly glad that I did not have to share their love. When I married in my adult years, I looked forward to the children we would have. Our first born, Chay, was four when Jamie was born, and he had enjoyed that only child status. When I stroked my growing belly, beginning to feel the movement that identified a new and unique life, I wondered how Chay's displacement as "only" would impact my young son as well.

In those days, we couldn't elect to know the sex of a soon-to-be-baby. The technology had not yet emerged. It was quite clear from this new child's in-utero activity that he was quite different in character from our first son. This baby seemed to be constantly active, and the vigor of his kicks should have given me a clue of his later football career. Chay, on the other hand, hardly moved at all during my pregnancy. If he had not been the first child so that I had no comparison, I might have really worried that the baby was not active. Later, when we saw what a scholar Chay became, we teased him that he was probably curled up with a book throughout the pregnancy.

I ended up with a Caesarean section when I had Chay. The labor was long, and after twenty-four hours, both the baby and I were exhausted. When his heart rate slowed dangerously, we were rushed into the ER for an emergency Caesarean. So when the obstetrician and I talked of the birthing arrangements for our second child, he offered me a choice. I could try to have the baby naturally or opt for another section. Since I had enjoyed natural childbirth classes in anticipation of Chay, I initially thought I would like to put them to use with this next baby. But a week before my due date, I awoke one morning with an overwhelming feeling that I should have another

C-section. The feeling was so intense that I decided that I had to allow it to guide me. When Jamie was born with the umbilical cord wrapped around his throat three times, I understood my premonition. He never would have survived a natural birth.

I should not have worried about my ability to love my second child, Jamie. Charlie, the oldest of six, had assured me that I needn't worry, as he was sure I had enough love for them both. From the very moment that eager little mouth attached itself firmly to my breast on the delivery table, Jamie and I connected. In fact, my mother cautioned me to include Chay as I was so caught up in caring for our new child. I am not sure if my older son's initial jealousy was a response to my total absorption in caring for Jamie or if it was just the typical response of a displaced "only" at the birth of a sibling. Chay suggested several times that it would be nice if "we sent the new baby back to where he came from."

Fortunately, Charlie was correct in his prediction and as I settled into mothering two children instead of one, Chay too began to embrace his baby brother. He would often alert me to things that he thought I should be doing for Jamie. "I think he needs a new diaper!" "Is he hungry?" Jamie was born with enlarged adenoids that caused him to snuffle in his sleep. One quiet afternoon while Jamie napped in another room, Chay, who had been playing nearby, commented: "Mommy, I hear something. It's either a pig or Jamie."

Despite the fact that I enjoyed my career as a college professor, I can honestly say that I was never happier than when caring for our two young sons. Like Chay's had been, Jamie's was a summer birth—early July—and I had a wonderful relaxing rest of the summer to enjoy the children before I returned to the college and work. The high point of that summer as every summer, was that we all spent some time at our summer cabin with my mom and dad, who enjoyed the boys as much as I did.

I had determined to continue breast-feeding after I returned to teaching when the summer ended and had arranged with my department chairman for a secluded office where I could express milk to prepare for the next day. Between classes, I retreated to my hideaway–an excursion jokingly termed by one of my female colleague friends as my "infant nutrition project." I managed to keep up my project throughout the school year. Eventually, my mother–from a different era when nursing was not as common in her circle–wondered light-heartedly if Jamie would still be nursing when he went off to college.

While I worked, a wonderful woman in town cared for Jamie and Chay–who spent part of his morning at a Montessori preschool and the afternoons at her home. I always felt confident that, in my absence at work, the children were well-cared for and happy with Mary. Life fell into a pattern. Charlie, the boys, and I spent some wonderful times together as a family, at home, on outings, and on family trips. I remember it as a happy time.

Our children manifested markedly different souls. Chay was endearing and outgoing, loved by all. Jamie was more active, but when he was ready to rest, it was to my side that he retreated, sometimes hiding behind me and almost seeming shy. While Chay often had his nose in a book right from the beginning, Jamie was the outdoors child, preferring to explore the yard and, in summer, the cabin. He had a voracious appetite for all life.

There are special times etched in my memory as I look back on Jamie and Chay's childhoods. In my own childhood, my parents and I discovered a whole series of books by Frank Baum tucked away in the attic of one of the houses they bought. We resurrected them, dusted them off, and, when we again moved, took the precious old books to the cabin for safekeeping.

The books made up the Oz series, and I loved them. While most children know only of Dorothy's trip to Oz via a tornado, I—and later my children—would be treated to many more of Dorothy's adventures, each more exciting than the previous.

I am reminded of my mother, Chay, and Jamie cuddled up on one of the beds at our one room cabin. With wide-eyed wonder and rapt attention, the boys listened as my mom read a bedtime story from one of the Oz books. I finished up the dinner dishes listening to every word and loving my children's reactions of delight. My own favorite was about Gingar, the female general whose all-girl army sported knitting needles as weapons. I often marveled at how Baum, rooted in his own time in the early 1900s, nonetheless wrote about empowered women.

Perhaps those times at the cabin were what would foster Jamie's great love for our haven in the Berkshires. From the bedtime stories to catching polliwogs in the nearby brook or sneaking up on unsuspecting beavers as they built their lodge and fished the pond they had created or toasting marshmallows during evenings by the fire, we cherished the children's development as they savored all the new experiences they encountered.

I find not only pictures of the cabin and our family events, but also some of Jamie at school and in church. One picture gives a chuckle; there is little Jamie dressed as an angel for the church Christmas pageant. An angel, indeed! Jamie who had been a dickens as a small child—not naughty, but devilish in cute ways, often teasing his big brother.

Church and Sunday School were integral parts of our lives throughout Jamie's childhood. As the daughter of a minister, I could not remember a time when I had not attended church. Chay and Jamie went to Sunday School from nursery through high school and obviously absorbed the teachings of love and kindness to others. Even though my boys were not as close as some brothers and sometimes had their differences like most siblings, there was never a meanness about their interactions. Each had an abundance of friends, which told me they knew how to interact positively with others.

Putting aside the early albums, I leaf through others trying to find photos I might include in a collage at his funeral.

Often, I find a picture of Jamie that includes some type of animal. Every cat and dog gravitated toward him. He loved all animals and often begged to bring home strays. Although I usually concluded that we had enough of a menagerie to care for, Jamie persevered in his attempts at rescues. At home, it was not uncommon to find him on his bed reading, a cat curled up beside him. His special favorite in his teen years was Aurora, a huge gray cat that arrived when he was five years old and departed the world peacefully when Jamie was in Bosnia, although he begged for her to hold on until he got home.

"You can't let Aurora die," he wrote. "I have to have a chance to say goodbye!"

Jamie claimed that Aurora was his counselor when, as a teenager, he struggled to deal with his parents' divorce.

"I talked to her for hours," he once told me, "and she really seemed to understand."

I remember well going into Jamie's room and finding him perched on the upper bunk of his bed with the huge grey cat snuggled against him. The psychologist in me understood that the cat had a special and important role in Jamie's life. At sixteen, Jamie found the conflicting emotions he had about his father's and my separation and later divorce difficult to process. Discussing his feelings with one of us may have seemed too much like disloyalty to the other parent. His happy-go-lucky, all-boy facade with his friends probably made it difficult for him to confess his true feelings to them either. Thus, he sought the company and perhaps unspoken counsel of his old cat, whose large yellow eyes could seem unusually intent and perceptive and who just listened, never offering advice.

And then there was teenaged Jamie with his dog, Molly, a rather willful German Shepherd-Husky cross who only had eyes for him. For our son, Molly was docile and obedient, but she let any other member of the family know she had no intention of being fully housebroken nor obeying. I helped my parents raise dogs when I was a child, and Molly's behavior constituted quite a blow for me. My childhood dogs and I entered shows and obedience trials. A beautiful dog that looked more German Shepherd than Husky, Molly posed in one picture at Jamie's feet looking like the model, devoted pet. When Jamie left for the Army, Molly grieved and was even more difficult, chewing up anything she could find, barking incessantly, and making us all wish he could have taken her with him.

Jamie's special animal love was wolves. He considered the wolf his animal totem. "People don't understand wolves," he often told me. "Wolves are loving and loyal but have gotten a really bad rep." How prophetic his words would later seem. I often wondered if it was Molly's wolf-like appearance that endeared her to Jamie.

Some pictures show Jamie at our cabin with whatever animal we had at the time. Any animal that was part of our family when summer rolled around spent time at the cabin. Cats, dogs, and birds all joined us. But Jamie also found woodland creatures to watch and engage with—a pet baby mouse rescued when we tired of its parent raiding our kitchen and trapped it. Jamie found a nest the mouse had left and tried to rescue the babies. Only one lived, and watching Jamie's devotion to it, I secretly wondered about the absurdity of saving the offspring after we had killed its parent. But the little mouse soon succumbed as well. Jamie carefully buried it in the yard with a special ceremony.

Jamie loved the woods and especially our cabin in the seclusion of the wooded Berkshires. My parents bought the cabin when I was three years old, and I spent summers there. My family drove all the way across the United States when we moved to California just to enjoy our restful summer haven. I remember those special road trips East well, metaphorically fueled as they were by our excited anticipation of being at the cabin again.

When I had children of my own, it felt natural to summer with them in the place I loved. By then, I was back in Massachusetts and only several hours from my summer paradise. Jamie, with his love of the outdoors, took to the cabin even more eagerly than his brothers. As a child, he loved spending summers there. Even as an older teen, he drove his car there to camp out alone, to bask in the solitude of his favorite place. If there was ever talk of inheritance, Jamie insisted that his brothers could have everything else. All he wanted was the cabin.

As I continue my perusal of photos, I find other pictures—pictures that bring me back from the joy of the cabin to more recent times. Here are pictures taken while Jamie was in basic training and even in Bosnia. It is a shock to see him dressed in camouflage posed with a gun half his size—so unlike my mind's pictures of my son. Seeing my son looking so comfortable with a gun brings me up short. Guns were not a part of my own upbringing, and I will admit being a bit afraid of them and what they represented to me—death and destruction. But when I first saw those pictures, I told myself that the big gun was part of his military training. Jamie told me that was one more tool to help him protect the country that he loved. Some photos from his military training show a more light-hearted Jamie joking with his buddies. I could imagine how much their friendship had meant to him.

One picture from Bosnia strikes me. Here is Jamie surrounded by a sea of Bosnian children—a lone GI looked up to by small members of the country where he served. Jamie often talked of the children in

Bosnia. He worried about their futures and hoped they could learn something other than war and violence.

Perusing pictures helps me very much in the week following Jamie's death. They let me remember good times, times of tenderness and love—a sharp contrast to the pain-filled reality that so starkly faced me. Even those taken during Jamie's military career gave me a picture of his life—a life I wanted to remember and savor.

Kaleidoscope of Shards

As we begin to make arrangements for his memorial service, the reality of his death begins to sink in. There are painful interrogations by police—both by those from the nearby town where he killed himself and by the state police.

Late afternoon on the day we learn of Jamie's death, Charlie, Jim, and I are summoned to the police station in the town where Jamie's death occurred. Town police and a state police officer confront us. While the town police officer we meet with is caring and gentle, the state police officer assigned to us is anything but. It seems just a duty to him. I recognize now—although my egocentric pain at the time may have prevented me from accepting the fact— that he was investigating a crime and a death. His dehumanization of all of us is nonetheless painful. I feel bludgeoned by his staccato questioning.

"Did you know where your son was that morning? What did he say to you the night before? Did he tell you where he was going?"

Bang! Bang! Bang! Penetrating my consciousness so that I wish I could somehow shield myself.

His questions of Jamie's dad, Charlie, of my husband, Jim, and of me make us feel more like guilty parties than bereft parents who cannot believe the nightmare we are living. He is brusque almost to the point of rudeness. He is definitely accusatory, suggesting that we have somehow been complicit or at least knew of Jamie's intent before the crime. I wonder if he has children or if he has any idea how much we all are in pain. It also seems that he wants this case to be simple—an open and shut love triangle, as I would later learn that the press was calling it. It is as if he wants to clean the case up as soon as possible.

I would later learn that he was also the investigator in a much-publicized child abduction case from many months before. And on the same weekend, police believed they found the body of the tragically killed young girl. Had I known it when he questioned us, perhaps I would have more compassion for the difficult cases he covered. But at the time it made me angry that he seemed to dismiss someone so important to me—my son—as a common criminal.

Jamie's story begins to unfold to our unbelieving ears. The trooper informs us with brutal certainty that Jamie had stolen a small knife from my kitchen—did I even realize it was missing—and used it to break into the lock on the door of the town police station near our home. According to the trooper, he stole a gun and went to the home in a nearby town where he broke into a house and threatened his former girlfriend and her current partner before taking his own life.

No! This was not my son who loved people and went out of his way to help others. He was not someone who would threaten others, and I thought I knew that he had no animosity toward his former girlfriend. He told me he hoped she had moved on and was happy. This could not be a story of the young man I had nurtured and in whom I had such high hopes. It cannot be true. I cannot imagine him threatening or harming anyone. I tried to block out the interrogator's words by denying that they constituted more than his erroneous theorizing. But still his questions came at us in brutal succession almost more swiftly than we could form answers.

"How long had he known the girl?" an officer barked.

"The girl?"

Ah, yes, the girl. My mind spins with memories blocking out the painful interview. The girl who had played such a significant role in his death had once held a place in my heart too.

"I've met someone, Mom," Jamie's words echoed somewhere in memory. "Why don't you come out to Fort Riley for Mother's Day, and you can meet her."

And what a wonderful Mother's Day it had been despite the almost unbearable heat of a Kansas May. Jamie had been living with his girl, and I wondered how I would feel about meeting a young woman who had captured my son's heart. She was lovely, I mused when we met, reminding me of a much-loved blonde-haired doll I had as a child. I called the doll Gwendolyn – which soon became shortened to Gwen—and delighted in her beautiful painted features and ability to walk and blink her eyes. She gave me many hours of joy. Was it this memory of a doll I cherished that so resembled Jamie's girl, my deep desire to have a daughter of my own, or this young woman's obvious attempts to please that won my own heart? Whatever the reason, I quickly grew to appreciate what Jamie saw in her. And as time has passed, I remember her more as Gwen than by her actual name. Perhaps it is my mind's need to idealize those positive feelings rather than face those that I would later feel about this girl.

During the week I stayed in their apartment, I basked in the glow of Jamie and Gwen's apparent happiness together. I had never seen Jamie in love before, and it warmed me. His eyes sparkled when he looked at her; at the same time, he included me in his admiration. I could tell it was important to him that I like his new love. He had girlfriends in the past, but this girl was clearly special.

I reluctantly parted from them and hoped Gwen would visit us. I had no idea that, although I saw an idyllic picture, sometimes things were far from good between them.

When the first four years of Jamie's eight-year enlistment ended, he decided to fulfill the remaining years by serving as a reservist while he went to college. Since the military was not yet deploying troops in any great number to Iraq in the spring of 2002, Jamie reasoned he could easily go to college from home. Remaining on active duty and taking classes when he could fit them in would have been difficult if not impossible.

Knowing that Jamie and Gwen were still a couple, I offered to bring her to our home where she could stay while she found an apartment and a job. Jamie had arranged to live with some former high school classmates near the college some seventy miles away where he had been accepted. Less enthusiastically than I had expected, Jamie agreed I should invite his girl. I extended the invitation, and Gwen excitedly planned with us when she would come.

As the time for her arrival drew near, Jamie admitted he did not want her to come. I wondered why his feelings had changed so suddenly. Had the glow that I had seen between the two young people been a byproduct of Jamie's being away from home—the same type of entanglement that forms a summer romance that fades with the return to routine that fall brings? Perhaps I should have explored his feelings further, but instead I counseled him with:

"It might be a disappointment to her, but if you don't want her here, it is only fair that you tell her now."

"I couldn't hurt her like that," he insisted. "She has her heart set on coming. She sees this as a new start." What followed was one of our many mother-son talks where he told me that he had hoped to "save" her. He explained that her childhood had been turbulent and fraught with abuse and substance abuse.

"I just want Gwen to know that there is something else—that families can be happy and care about each other," he explained. "Just let her come. I'll be at college anyway."

My mind drifted back to the stray animals Jamie had been so desperate to shelter. Was my loving son once more intent on being the rescuer? There was something about Gwen when I met her—an air of neediness covered by a somewhat seductive vibrato and a joking manner that was her allure. Had Jamie been taken in by being far away but now—in the safety of his home where he felt safe, loved, and familiar—did he see more clearly what may have been an infatuation built on sand?

As I listened to my son talk about how it was only fair to follow through with our invitation to the girl, I recognized that he was an adult—someone who had spent four years in the Army making his own decisions and fighting his own battles—both literally and emotionally. Despite my conflicts about Jamie's ambivalence, I knew that, as his mother, I had to respect his wishes. So with great trepidation and against the advice of my closest friend, Kate, to whom I had confessed my reservations, I made good on my invitation and brought the young woman into our home.

It would change our lives forever.

The voice of the trooper insinuates itself into my consciousness and erases the brief escape into memory.

"You can go," he barks. "Contact me if you have further information." He thrusts a business card at me. I flinch and pull back. Someone else—Charlie, perhaps—takes it from him. That trooper's face and his rapid-fire questions haunt my nightmares for weeks.

I feel numb on the ride home—Jim and me in our car, since Charlie had come alone. Jim says little, and I cannot form any words to describe how I feel. I just want to get home into the sanctuary where my son had grown up and where our memories of happier days and our love for him resided, a place where I can hear his voice and envision the youth I loved so well. I need to bask in positive remembrances as we prepare to say our final goodbye to the young man we loved and remembered.

Splintered Reflections

Days later, I had almost finished assembling the photo album for Jamie's memorial service when I found the fresh envelope of pictures. On top of the pile was the one of Jamie, his girl, Gwen, and me at the lake that Mother's Day. It had been a gorgeous but very windy day with the large lake breaking into waves as gusts hit the shore. Joking about having an ocean in Kansas, we cavorted through the waves. It was a time of love and laughter.

Other pictures chronicled the fun we had soon after she came to live with us. In one picture, Jamie and Gwen perch on a deck overlooking scenic Gloucester Harbor in Massachusetts. Another captures autumn leaves cascading around them as they frolic on a weekend Jamie spent at home during college. I put those pictures away. I found it too painful to see the three of us in such moments of happiness.

I busied myself with plans for the memorial service. I had decided I would write his eulogy. It was something I had to do for my son—or was it for myself? Was I stealing the moment to say the goodbye fate had cheated from me? As I reviewed my son's short life, I marveled at his uniqueness. How fortunate we were to have had twenty-two years with him. I thought again of the fact that, had I not chosen to have Jamie by Caesarean section, we could have lost him.

A lover of country music, I would later hear Garth Brooks mirror my feelings in his song "The Dance":

> And now I'm glad I didn't know
> The way it all would end, the way it all would go.
> Our lives are better left to chance.
> I could have missed the pain,
> But I'd have had to miss the dance.

I would not have wanted to miss the dance of love, that precious mother-son bond.

Now it was time to remember the years of the dance and grieve that it had ended.

The memorial service would be in the Community Church of North Orange and Tully where I had done a required internship as a seminary student. I came to love that church in a nearby village. I had grown to feel a part of the church family and had special affection for the pastor, Reverend Lois. When I completed my internship, I joined the church community. I knew the church people there would share my grief and help us say a meaningful goodbye to Jamie.

As we prepared for the memorial, I went over last-minute details with Jeff Cole, the funeral director. I selected the funeral home with care and chose to make the arrangements alone. I had worked with Jeff while I was a student minister, and I loved his gentle manner with people. I remembered watching him as he took care to meet the needs of people devastated by loss. I had confidence that Jeff's way of caring would be a balm for me, too.

I would not be disappointed. As Jeff and I talked of Jamie's life to gather material for the obituary, Jeff listened with tender compassion. He helped me cope with the difficult decisions that Jamie's father and I had to make. I went alone to this meeting with Jeff. I am not sure why Charlie was not with me. Perhaps it was something that I needed to do alone. Our joint decisions would come later.

And then it was time for me to have a private goodbye with my son before calling hours opened that privilege to friends and the rest of the family.

I had given Jeff my favorite of Jamie's outfits to dress him for the last time. The casual pants and off-white Irish knit turtleneck sweater contrasted with his dark hair and blue eyes so he looked the epitome of the Celtic lad he was. I knew he would approve of his burial attire. He had died during his years as a soldier and took pride in that role, but I somehow knew that what I had chosen for his last appearance to others would please him more than being laid out in his military regalia.

As Jeff ushered me into the parlor where Jamie lay in a coffin, I was at first shocked to see my vibrant son so still. Jeff quietly excused himself, and Jamie and I were alone.

I have heard mourners complain that their loved one does not look like himself when displayed for a funeral. Whether because of the skill of the embalmer or the loving lens of my mother eyes, Jamie looked like my Jamie, child of my heart. Long eyelashes the envy of his female friends were obvious with his eyes closed as if in slumber. Imagining him playing one more game, I tucked his football beside him. Tears blurred my sight as I gazed upon the peaceful, still body of my son.

"Why, Jamie?" I whispered. "Why did you do it? You always seemed to love life." But no answer emerged from my son's motion-less lips. No, I thought, how he died is not something I wanted to think about. It is how he lived that I would cherish.

I touched his face and was stunned by how cold it was. I imagined that, at any moment, he would break into a smile: I rarely saw my son without one. His friends would later tell me that Jamie was known for that brilliant, engaging smile. His smile was so expansive that it seemed every tooth was visible. I chuckled as I remembered the photographer who took his picture when he was three.

"Smile, Son!" he had intoned. And then he laughed "My, you have—a lot of teeth!"

But this Jamie before me was somber compared to the son I knew in life. Yet he also looked at peace, and I thanked God that whatever demons had plagued his last days, he was now free of them. As I said a final goodbye to my beloved son, I choked out the words, "I love you, Jamie. You will always be the child of my heart."

Calling hours that evening were a tribute to the life my son had led and the lives he had touched. As his local friends processed by us, many reintroducing themselves because four years since high school graduation had changed and matured them, I could only imagine how they must feel. One does not often lose a peer so early in life. No doubt also relieved that they were not in our places, family and friends offered support and sympathy. I was touched when Dana, one of our town police officers, filed past with his wife. Dana was the son of Mary who cared for Jamie in infancy, and the fact that he was a police officer mattered. Despite the manner of my son's death, Dana responded to our need to remember him. I would never forget his presence there on that day and how much it meant to me.

Others expressed their concern in unique ways. I remember Chris, Jamie's closest friend, keeping a careful watch out for Gwen.

"She wouldn't dare show up, would she?" his friends whispered. They saw the girl as instrumental in Jamie's death. Those friends knew, too, that the family would find her presence especially hurtful. I later learned that we should not have worried. Gwen had left the area the night of Jamie's death—though given that she was a witness to the events of that night, I never understood how the police allowed her to leave.

Somehow, we—Jamie's family—endured the evening of calling hours. At its end, though exhausted by the mantle of grief so heavy upon our shoulders, we were all touched by sentiments expressed by so many. Knowing he would then be taken for cremation, as was his wish, I gazed at my son one last time.

"I want my ashes scattered at the cabin," he once told me, perhaps in a moment of premonition. I remember thinking that I, too, wanted the cabin to be my final resting place, the cabin where we all loved to relax and be at peace with nature. Even though my other sons loved the cabin, it was Jamie who spoke of having a soul connection with it and the surrounding woods.

"He was loved," my mother said softly as she put an arm around me and bringing me back to the present. I knew that Mom had not been feeling well, an ailment that doctors would later diagnose as cancer, and yet here she was comforting me. I had placed a chair beside me so she could also greet people. She had risen weakly in an effort to nurture her child as we together grieved mine.

"Indeed, he was," I responded, urging her to sit back down.

The number of mourners attested to Jamie's popularity. Pain on the faces of his young peers, especially, told me how much they had loved him.

Another country song, "Three Wooden Crosses," flashed through my mind as it would many times during the days and months to come.

> I guess it's not what you take
> when you leave this world behind you,
> it's what you leave behind you
> when you go.

The song ran through my head as my family and I greeted other mourners at the Community Church the next day, lovely in May. Watching people file into the church from my spot on the front lawn, I savored the sun's warmth. I thought it too beautiful a day for saying goodbye.

I saw a few faces from Jamie's high school class I had not seen at the calling hours. They looked older than I remembered as they milled about, seemingly unsure of what to do. Despite the progression of years, they seemed very young. Suddenly, I remembered their senior year at Fitchburg's Saint Bernard's High School when football team members hung together so closely. Jamie spoke often of the young men who joined together in the common goal of playing football to win the high school Super Bowl. Jamie played every game that year.

I remembered the awards banquet when his teammates let Jamie know how they felt about him. Jamie had a mind of his own and sometimes questioned his coach. I suspect Jamie's teammates liked him better than his coach did. Jamie's teammates knew they could depend on Jamie to offer words of encouragement and praise for jobs well done. Because the team won the Super Bowl trophy that year, we football parents took great pride in all of our sons.

On the night of the sports awards banquet at the end of each school year, coaches honored players who had played every game that season. The coaches did not choose Jamie, who had braved all types of weather to play at every game. Presentations continued, and we heard an undertone among the football players. Several got up and had their own huddle in the hall. When they returned, they did not look pleased. I am not sure if it happened that night or in the days following the banquet, but one of Jamie's friends told us that, all together, his teammates confronted the coaches to right the wrong. Jamie eventually received an apology and appropriate recognition several days later, but I found it sad that the coaches disappointed our son. As we drove home from the awards banquet that night, he talked about this teammate or that, and I wondered how he hid his disappointment. That was Jamie's way—to praise his teammates' efforts and minimize his own.

"It is hard to believe that he is gone," I heard someone whisper to someone else, thus interrupting me from my memories.

As I moved into the church sanctuary for the memorial service, I noticed chairs set up in the church hall to accommodate overflow. I later learned that more than 250 mourners attended calling hours and perhaps more the memorial service.

Our family gathered in the first pew. My husband, Jim, who shared his appreciation for physical work with Jamie and saw Jamie as the son he had not had, looked as pained as I felt. I thought of the most recent projects that Jim and Jamie had worked on together—putting down stones on our front walk and building a shed at the cabin. I knew Jim hoped Jamie, with his love of the outdoors, would develop an interest in logging. Jim had mentioned how he dreamed of leaving the mill he had so laboriously built from nothing to Jamie, to run it eventually himself. That dream died with Jamie.

Jim reached out to take my hand in comfort as I sat down beside him. Jamie's dad, Charlie, took his place on my other side.

Our son Chay, who had come from California with his fiancée, Becky, was devastated by his brother's death. As children, Chay and Jamie may not have been particularly close, but as young adults, they had begun to forge a new and closer relationship. The close relationship ended suddenly, a very difficult fact for Chay. Andrew sat huddled close to my mother, who had always supported him and continued in this moment when his shattered parents could not offer him much solace. Knowing the service would soon begin I gathered my strength to offer the eulogy.

I glanced around the congregation. Although people filled every seat with more overflowing into the parish hall, the choir section at the front of the church remained empty. As the pastor rose to begin, a stirring commenced at the rear of the hall as a parade of clean-cut young men dressed in jackets and ties marched solemnly up the aisle and filled the choir section. I realized that the entire football team from Jamie's senior year at Saint Bernard's, accompanied by wives or girlfriends, had come together to say goodbye to their teammate. The young men, most fighting tears, joined together in tribute to their fallen teammate. Anyone in the congregation who had thus far held back tears lost the struggle at the sight of the grieving young people.

When the time came for me to speak, I somehow found strength to share with the mourners how Jamie's mother felt. In part, I told them:

> Jamie was deeply interested in Native American folklore and especially in animal totems. From early in his life, his special animal was the wolf. He often told me that he felt in harmony with this creature. Pictures and statues of wolves adorned every living space he inhabited from his room at home and his locker at school to his Army cubicle. I never fully understood the communion between Jamie and his wolves until I read a passage in one of his favorite books, *Animal Speak: The Spiritual and Magical Powers of Creatures Great and Small*. Let me share this passage with you.

> The wolf is the most misunderstood of animals. Tales of terror and their cold-bloodedness abound. In spite of their negative press, wolves are the exact opposite of how they are portrayed. They are friendly, social, and highly intelligent. Their sense of family is strong and loyal. Wolves are the epitome of the wild, the true spirit of the free and unspoiled wilderness. Their positive characteristics are so numerous that it is no wonder that the Native Americans and others practically deify them.

I finished the eulogy:

> And here we are today, saying farewell to a special young man, a philosopher, an idealist, a dreamer, an animal lover, a wonderful friend, and a beloved son. So, be in peace, Child of my Heart. My heart is broken now and part of it will always be with you.

Several of Jamie's friends offered their thoughts following my words. David, one of his football teammates, compared Jamie to Ajax, a figure of Greek mythology, a brave warrior who died falling on his sword.

I had not wanted to talk about how Jamie died—by his own hand. That was not what I wanted to think of, and it disturbed me that David brought what I considered ugliness into our midst. David meant well, I told myself. The young man had adored Jamie and perhaps he, too, felt disillusioned and confused by the manner of his death. But I listened to David's remarks and could see what he and Jamie shared. Both found meaning in the allegorical, and through their shared interest, David, deep in his own pain, sought understanding and comfort.

Jamie's closest friends, Chris and Sarah, reflected together on Jamie's life. They read beautiful, thoughtful excerpts from his letters to them and told of the times they spent together and how much they loved their fallen friend. Theirs had been a unique trio. I suspected that Jamie and Chris both loved the beautiful, warm Sarah, and their three-way relationship resonated with depth of mutual understanding. Now each of them talked of Jamie's sensitivity, his compassion, and especially his warm, smiling presence in their lives. Each of them could confide in him. His good-natured humor lifted them out of whatever crisis may have enveloped them. Sarah and Chris's sensitivity and grace attested to those same qualities in their friend.

One of Jamie's Army buddies traveled from southern Connecticut to pay tribute to his comrade. Barely able to speak through tears and sobs, the young soldier spoke of knowing Jamie in the military. He said Jamie was always there for his brothers in arms. The young soldier's stories and obvious grief moved the congregation.

We gathered for refreshments after the service, and the funeral director, Jeff, approached me. Looking tearful, he told me, "I never met Jamie, but through our time talking together and after witnessing today, I feel as if I knew him and would have wanted to be his friend." I hugged Jeff in thanks. Jamie was gone, but he had left behind him respect and love.

Losing the Way

The weeks before Jamie's unexpected death had not been easy. In February when we suggested a big celebration for Mom's eightieth birthday, she admitted she did not feel well and could eat very little. I noticed that she had lost weight, but I was involved in my clinical pastoral education placement at Saint Vincent's Hospital in Worcester and didn't pay it the attention I might have done.

After twenty-five years of college teaching, I had taken early retirement to finish seminary courses. Taking a few courses each semester while I taught full time, I began seminary 1997. I completed my field education at the North Orange Church while still teaching. But then I faced clinical pastoral education that would place me as a chaplain in a hospital setting. As a therapist for years and a full time social worker before that, I knew the demand of such work. So when the college offered an early retirement package, I took it, deciding to devote my full attention to preparing for the ministry.

I also had my mom to think of. My mother's admission of her condition led to a myriad of specialists' appointments in both Worcester and Boston, each an hour or more away by car, to discover why she could not eat and kept growing weaker. Experts could not come up with a diagnosis. All they agreed upon was that she did not have cancer, one of my fears after Mom's sister died from it.

Despite her efforts to support me in the days and weeks after Jamie's death, I could see my mother growing even weaker. She insisted she would be fine, but since she lived alone, I worried. I recognized that our loss of Jamie surely also must have affected her. My father had been a minister, and weighty theological and philosophical subjects were the norm around our house. Jamie, Mom, and I had enjoyed wonderful discussions about everything from the nature of the universe and roots of each of our faiths to what happens when you die. During a discussion about death, Jamie made his announcement that he wanted his ashes scattered at our cabin.

Jamie loved to hear stories of my father, who died when Jamie was only nine months old. Jamie carried Dad's name, so it seemed to follow that, like Dad, he loved deep discussions. Jamie felt he could have learned from my dad and regretted that his grandfather died before Jamie got to know him. In our discussions, we often remembered Gum, as our first two children called my dad due to Chay's inability as a toddler to say Gramps. During one reminiscence, Jamie said, "After I die, I picture myself sitting at Gum's feet and just listening to him."

That comment gave my mother much joy, and she frequently mentioned it. A week or so after Jamie's death, my mother said, "I can just imagine Jamie with your Dad. The discussions they could have!"

I chuckled. When I allowed myself to believe that Jamie had actually died, I also thought of him enjoying my father's company. Even now, I imagine them together with a rich relationship.

Just before Jamie's death, I had finished seminary courses for the year and my pastoral care placement. I then had a chance to turn my thoughts to my mother's illness. We didn't know what to explore next in our pursuit of a diagnosis. Jamie's death and the immediate following days caused us to reschedule several tests from May to early June.

How painful to see my mother in obvious ill health. She had always served as the rock in my life, the person I could turn to when I felt my world on shaky ground. She supported me through divorce and becoming a single parent for three children, one of them with special needs. She spent much of her time helping with Andrew's care, allowing me to work and support the family.

More than the support Mom offered me, we had a special, dear relationship. For a while, she and my dad lived in Florida, and I dreamed of having them close so that we could visit and they could be involved with our children. When my father died, Mom had built a life in Florida, so she stayed there. But characteristic of our relationship, my mother dropped everything and moved back to Massachusetts when Andrew's needs became all consuming. Finally, she lived close by, and we had the loving relationship in my adulthood that I had long dreamed of.

I watched Mom as she tried valiantly to support me as I ached at losing Jamie. And I could see what it had done to her. I would later realize that her grief multiplied as she not only mourned the loss of her grandson but suffered as she watched her only child's pain.

In the weeks after Jamie's death, we all tried simply to hold on. I worked to busy myself with all that needed to be accomplished, but I felt barely able to put one foot in front of the other.

Chay and Becky returned to their home in California. They planned to marry that September and wondered if they should go ahead with their plans. We told them that we all needed a wedding as contrast to our grief. Andrew went back to the residential treatment center, and I worried that he did not seem to be grieving. His therapist assured us that he would do so as time passed but it was too difficult for Andrew to comprehend in the immediate days following Jamie's death.

My husband, Jim, returned to work, and in his characteristically stoic way tried to cope with the loss of the young man he had hoped would inherit the sawmill that Jim had so lovingly built and operated. I knew that Jamie's dad, Charlie, also suffered. Although Charlie and I talked, we had not completely healed from a difficult divorce, and I did not know how to help him.

So we each went about our lives, each encased in personal grief and having difficulty knowing how to give real comfort to each other. What a barren time, after the death of someone you love. After finishing all the casseroles of comfort and after mourners depart to their own business once more, you are left alone with your family for comfort.

I could not imagine who or what would comfort me. Nothing seemed to ease the pain or fill that empty space where death wrenched my child from my heart.

We had no real plans for the Memorial Day just weeks after Jamie's death. Then came the call that would further change our lives.

"I fell this morning," my mother's frail voice admitted almost sheepishly. "I just couldn't get myself up, and it frightened me. I thought I had better call an ambulance." My alarm at her words revealed as much about the unlikelihood of her reaching out for help—let alone an ambulance—as the fact that she had fallen.

"I'll be right there." I said, grabbing my keys.

"No," she said urgently. "Come to the hospital. I'm going there."

"Do you want me to go?" asked Jim as I explained quickly on my way out the door.

"No. I'll call you when I know what's up."

When I reached the hospital in nearby Athol, Mom had already been admitted. It was hard to imagine that only months before she had been an active, independent, and strong woman. Now she looked anything but.

"I need to figure out what's going on," she told me weakly. "I want to be at Chay's wedding."

Ah, yes. Chay and Becky's wedding only four months away in September. I prayed she would get well by then.

Over the next few days, doctors conferred about how to proceed. Mom was weak but nonetheless cheerful. One morning, I went to visit her, and she mentioned she had had the strangest dream.

"I dreamed I was on a subway in Boston," she said.

Knowing how much she hated both going into Boston and the subway, I chuckled.

"Then Jamie got on," she continued. "He looked just the same, in that white sweater we all loved on him. And he said 'Move over, Nana. I'm here with you now. We can ride together.'"

Ever the caring Jamie, I thought, even after death. Mom wondered what the dream meant. I pushed it from my thoughts as a nurse interrupted our musing with some news.

An ambulance would take Mom to the specialist's office to keep her previously scheduled appointment. I cannot remember the doctor's specialty nor where his office was except in a nearby town. I don't remember why I did not go with her, as was my custom. Perhaps Mom assured me that she would rather go alone, or more likely, hospital or ambulance company policy prevented me from riding in the ambulance with her. I did see her into the ambulance and went home to await the news.

Later, the hospital called and asked me to come in for a conference.

When I reached the hospital, Mom waited in a wheelchair.

"I think you should be prepared," she told me.

"Why?" I asked in concern. "Have they told you something?"

"No . . ." Her voice trailed off as I pushed her wheelchair to the room where we would have our meeting. She had grown too weak to walk—something that should have prepared me.

The concerned but solemn look on the doctor's face told me all I needed to know.

No doubt recognizing the impact his words would have, he said in a kind and caring voice, "It is cancer."

"But they said it wasn't cancer!" I rushed to explain as if that fact would negate his findings.

"I am sorry, but it is. It began in the ovaries but has metastasized throughout the body. There is nothing we can do." He spoke with calm authority.

"Nothing!" It was a demand, a challenge. They could do nothing? This could not be happening. I would not let it happen. I could not lose my mother. Not now. I think I had started to argue when I felt my mother's soft hand on my arm.

"How long?" she asked in a surprisingly steady voice.

"Weeks, a month," the doctor told us.

I remember little about the rest of my visit with my mother. We must have talked about the diagnosis—or maybe we didn't. We were both stunned. The doctor had just confirmed all of our worst fears. We weren't ready to think or plan. We simply tried to digest the news of the death sentence Mom had just received.

Mom said she was tired and suggested I go home, that we would talk in the morning. Like a robot, I drove home. Not until I got home and Jim asked anxiously what had happened did I break into tears. After Jamie's death, I thought I had no tears left, but now they flowed. I wasn't sure I could ever stop.

"She'll come here with us," Jim said, taking charge when he knew that I could not. "We'll get a hospital bed and make the den into a bedroom. That way there will be no stairs, and we'll be here for her."

I could not believe what I heard. I had been married to this man for only four short years, and here he was willing to turn over our lives for my dying mother. I have never felt more grateful to him.

When I told her, my mom took the news quietly. Finally she said, "You can't do that. The summer is your writing time. You have a book due." Her response was almost comical. Yes, when I was a college professor, I used summers at the cabin to write the books that had become my income. How many summers had Mom entertained the children in the morning while I wrote, then fixed us lunch? After lunch, we did something together like go swimming or some other fun activity. My schedule depended on my mother, whose commitment to the children had allowed me to write.

Secretly thinking I would not have the psychic energy to write under the circumstances, I assured her, "I'll get the writing done. Are you going to keep me hopping every minute?" At least I could tease her, if only feebly.

The first few days after we brought Mom to our home that next Sunday, she had all she could do to get out of bed and take liquids and soft foods. I tried to find food that would taste good to her.

We liked to observe that, in our family, neither my mom nor I coped well with illness. Both active and usually healthy, we had no tolerance for illness in ourselves. Both of us could be sympathetic to others with illness, but taking time to be sick ourselves didn't work for us.

I remember once visiting my mom at her Florida home. I promptly got a gastrointestinal virus that fortunately lasted only a few days. When it was obvious I was on the mend, she came into my room one morning with a bright and cheery smile. "So," she said, "am I going to change the bed or are you going to lie there being sick?"

When I told the story later, some listeners may not have understood that the comment had us both laughing and eased my sick time. Of old Yankee stock, she did what she had to do no matter the challenges. On the other hand, there was no one more caring than my mother, especially where the children or I were concerned.

I wondered about my own ability to care for someone lying ill or dying, but I need not have worried. My love for my mom made the burden light, and I found myself consumed with finding ways to make her more comfortable. My mother's mantra, on the other hand, was "When are you going to write?"

That week after she came to our house was a precious time for us. When she was awake and able, we talked and talked. We looked over the many cards people had sent us when Jamie died. We talked about our memories of him and the other children when they were little. Mom shared more of her own memories of childhood. We both knew we shared our memories in the guise of saying goodbye, and it felt right. I had brought Mom's two cats from her house to give her comfort, and they took turns on her bed. Ebony especially loved to warm her feet.

As the week progressed, Mom grew weaker. She could no longer get out of bed, and she slept quite a bit. Visits from hospice workers punctuated our days. When they were not tending to her, I spent most of my time by Mom's bed. It was where I wanted to be. Despite her illness, Mom clearly worried about me. Remembering that the dying often need permission to go, I assured her I would be okay. But I could not bear to see her go.

The Sunday a week after Mom came home to us, she was very weak. She urged me to go to church, which I did reluctantly. I hurried home to find her sleeping peacefully. Reverend Lois, a great friend of my mother's, visited her in the afternoon and wondered if I felt I could take part in an evening service at the church.

"I think I need to be here," I told her, and she understood.

That early evening, my mom and I talked a bit, although it was more and more difficult for her. Thinking how frail she had become, I sat stroking her hand. I thought back on all the times she had been there for me—how strong she had been and what a wonderful model of strength I had found in her.

"You know," I said to her, "you have always been the wind beneath my wings," referring to the popular song we both loved.

"And I always will be," she responded weakly. Her eyes closed. She drifted to sleep. Feeling her shallow breath as her chest rose and fell, I kissed her and went to the kitchen when I heard the whistle of the kettle I had put on earlier for tea. My tea made, I returned to Mom's side. Ebony, the cat curled around her feet, glanced up at her and jumped from the bed. I gazed at my mother's face, and I knew, just as the cat had known seconds before, that she was gone.

Aware that I must call hospice and the funeral home, I sat beside her bed for a time. Mundane details would wait. Despite the June warmth, I felt a chill and cold and very much alone.

When Jamie died, I felt that I had lost a bit of my future—for aren't children the legacy you leave as part of the ongoing progression of life? Certainly, I had two other children, and each is unique in his own way and therefore irreplaceable as Jamie was irreplaceable—stamped by my influence and charged to carry that part of me into the generations to come. Losing my mother, however, constituted a different kind of loss.

As an only child with no siblings to share memories of childhood, I realized that, in my mother's death, I lost anyone who shared my past. I met Charlie when I was twenty-eight and married him soon after. Since my parents and I moved often when I was growing up, I maintained no relationships from childhood. It felt as if I had begun a new life at twenty-eight with only my parents to share previous memories. On this June day with my father long gone and my mother dead, my history slate wiped clean of remembrances shared with them. Although I could not say why, the realization came with a sense of feeling especially bereft.

The depth of despair I felt from losing Jamie deepened as I thought of the world without my mother. Not only my history and long-term future but the immediate days ahead seemed devoid of purpose. How could I keep going? Where would I find strength to face tomorrow and the next day? I wondered if I had the reserves to go on doing what I needed to do in my own life and for all of those I loved. I couldn't even cry. I had no energy to do even that.

Several days later, I once again found myself on the way home from the funeral home after talking with Jeff Cole about a memorial service. Feeling devoid of emotion as I drove, I noticed a field I passed whenever I went to town. The previous fall, it had been logged and the stumps removed. After winter snow melted, the field turned an ugly, muddy mess. Now in late June, it shown resplendent as bright yellow buttercups created a glorious blanket of color. What a miracle had transpired. From an ugly field, God created something of beauty—a balm for my soul so in need of healing. I wondered fleetingly if the God who transformed what I saw as an ugly field into something of such beauty could ever take my shattered dreams and injured spirit and create something half as wonderful as he had in that field.

Touching Bottom

In the weeks after Mom's death, I sank deeper and deeper into depression.

I considered how my mother refused to eat toward the end and thus hastened her death. She insisted she did not want to rob me of the time she felt I needed to write, and I suspected not eating was her way of giving me that time. But after she died, I found I could not concentrate on writing. I had a contract for a book, and for the first time in my writing career, I had to admit to my publisher that I would not finish on time. In fact, I had no idea when I could do it justice, as I did not have the emotional stamina to return to writing. The compassionate editor assured me the book would get finished when I could return to it.

I began grief-counseling sessions with the hospice therapist, Araya Fast, following Mom's death. A psychiatric social worker like me, Araya recognized that my complex grief related more in some ways to Jamie's death than my mother's. She continued to see me well after the time the hospice service would ordinarily end. As a therapist, I knew I had found a very competent colleague, and I valued our work together. Still, I didn't know why even such wise counsel could not lift me from the depth of my despair. When I finally began to heal, I thought back on counseling with her and realized how much she had helped. But in the midst of those early days, I could not fully see it.

And then came summer, the time of year I love the most, and I found no pleasure in it. The two small boxes sitting on my shelf, Jamie's ashes and Mom's ashes, constantly reminded me that those receptacles contained all that remained of them, except for my memories. I had planned to scatter the ashes, Jamie's at the cabin and Mom's near my Dad's grave in Florida, but I could not part with them. The last tangible pieces of the two people I loved seemed too precious to abandon to the elements.

Perhaps I would find solace at our cabin in the Berkshires, I told myself. So in late June, I asked Jim to open it with me. The shuttered cabin is always cold, dark, and musty when we open it after its winter slumber. I walked into the semi-darkness and headed for the service box to turn on the electricity while Jim worked on removing the outside shutters. As the lights illuminated the still-shuttered room, my heart skipped a beat as my glance fell on one of the beds.

There in a little pile were some things I knew to be Jamie's. A small notebook bore his tiny, neat script. Medicinal uses of herbs fascinated him, and as I flipped through the pages, I saw that he had apparently kept a record of various herbs. Several exceptionally beautiful feathers lay beside the book. A lover of Native American lore, Jamie collected feathers. As a teenager, he belonged to the Order of the Arrow in Boy Scouts and used his feathers to fashion his ceremonial costume. Later, he collected them for his own enjoyment.

There, too, I found a beaded choker that Jamie often wore, its intricate Native American pattern holding meaning that I did not understand. I took it in my hands imagining I could feel the warmth of my dear son who had worn it. Seemingly mundane amidst the pile of treasures I found his mess kit, the metal interlocking plate, bowl, and utensils that soldiers use in the field. With that I realized that Jamie had come to this place when he disappeared some nights in the months before he died. I had assumed he went to friends' houses, and trying to respect the push and pull of an adult son's need for autonomy and privacy, I had not asked where he went.

I wondered why Jamie had not removed shutters or opened the cabin up but instead apparently had camped in the dark solitude, perhaps attesting to his growing depression. Tearfully, I fastened the chocker around my own neck, surprised somehow that the beads felt cold. Lovingly, I placed the other items on a shelf above the bed and continued sweeping and cleaning to open the cabin while Jim took down the shutters to let in light.

As the one-room cabin brightened, I spied another remnant of Jamie's life on the old wooden desk that had been my father's for many years: a receipt for a round-trip e-ticket flight to Kansas in July, the next month. Instantly I understood and became overcome with recognition that my son *had* envisioned his future. The trip I knew would have enabled Jamie to stand as godfather to little Austin, born the previous September to his friends Ron and Amanda.

Jamie spoke often of his friend, Ron, who served with him in Bosnia and had become a close friend. Ron and Jamie had been stationed together at Fort Riley in Kansas. When Ron married a local woman, Amanda, Jamie was among the groomsman at their wedding. I remember Jamie's letters about the birth of Ron and Amanda's first baby, Taylor. Jamie waited expectantly in the waiting room during the birth and saw the infant Taylor as the first person to do so after her mom and dad. Thereafter, Taylor would be imprinted on Jamie's heart.

"She feels almost like my own child," he wrote home. "I never thought a baby could feel so special."

Amanda remembers the first time she was up after the birth and how Jamie—who had been at the hospital—walked with her.

"I dissolved in tears," she later told me, "because I saw in the mirror how awful I looked. But Jamie assured me I was beautiful, and that meant so much."

Jamie was thrilled when Ron and Amanda asked him to be godfather to little Taylor. My son looked forward to assuming that role. Each time he came home on leave, he looked for gifts to take back to Taylor. I remember him once buying her a huge stuffed bear that would easily have been twice her size. He resolved to take it back on the plane and had quite a discussion with the ticket agent who insisted that—were he to take it on the plane with him—he would have to buy an extra seat to accommodate the size. The airline staff finally agreed that he could check the animal, and Jamie did, reluctantly. I never learned but often wondered how Taylor reacted when he gave her the huge toy.

Jamie filled his letters home with news about Taylor and her parents. But then Gwen came into his life, and things changed. Jamie became so enmeshed in her spell that he ignored his friends' admonitions that she was not good for him. When friends persisted in their concern that she would hurt Jamie if he continued a relationship with her, he turned away from them.

I would not know all of it until after his death. Although he and his friends experienced temporary rifts, I remember the call the first September he was home telling him that Ron and Amanda had another child—a little boy. They asked Jamie to be Austin's godfather, too.

As I stood in our cabin with the ticket receipt in my hand, I knew that Jamie had had every intention of flying to Kansas to meet his newest godchild. What could have happened to make my son—filled with life and hope for the future—decide to end his life so tragically?

I spent some time alone at the cabin that summer. All around me, memories spoke of my childhood and summers spent there with Mom and Dad. I remembered the wooden hobby horses Dad had fashioned for me when I was a child and the delight on little Jamie's face when I unearthed them and gave them to him. The nearby brook seemed to echo sounds of laughter when Jamie and Chay hunted for polliwogs and chased water spiders. I thought of the German Shepherd my mom had: the dog so loved water that she would dash to and fro throwing water over her back to the delight of five-year-old Jamie, who laughed so hard that we feared he would fall off the rock where he perched to watch the show. Memories surrounded me like a warm cloak, but at the same time, they isolated me from the living.

Whether at the cabin or at home, I found it difficult to read after Jamie died. I could not possibly do the research necessary to write my book, let alone read anything for pleasure. If friends called and invited me to come over or go for a walk or to the movies, I made an excuse. I preferred to exist within my own cocoon of grief. I found pleasure in nothing and wanted no one. I thought of Jamie and wondered again and again if I could have prevented his death, even though as a therapist I fully knew the professional counsel that, when a person decides to commit suicide, no one else can influence the decision.

Late that summer, I mustered strength to scatter Jamie's ashes at our cabin, the place he loved so. I resolved that, in the winter, I would take my mother's ashes to Florida to place them near my father's grave.

As I opened the box that held Jamie's ashes, the white sand-like substance surprised me. It was all that remained of my son's physical body. I sifted the ashes through my fingers as I scattered them in his favorite places—near the outdoor fireplace, beside the brook, near the old swing. I tried to feel his warmth and remember the echo of his laughter.

"Goodbye, Child of My Heart. You will always be a part of me," I whispered.

In the end, I could not bear to scatter them all and kept a small amount sequestered in a wooden box with a picture of a wolf on top. I placed it near my bed in the cabin to greet me each summer to come.

I could not spend the entire summer at the cabin. Jim was working at home, and I owed him time, too. I had taken no seminary classes during the summer. I needed to gather my resources after the deaths. I am not sure what I did when I was not at the cabin. I should have been writing, but I did not have the strength or inspiration. I had my counseling office in a lovely old building near my house, but I had cut back on clients when I started my pastoral counseling internship that previous fall.

At home, I suppose I cooked meals and interacted with Jim, but I doubt that I did more otherwise than sit. My interaction with Jim was shallow at best. He, too, grieved, but his way of coping was to work even longer hours. I am sure that Charlie and I must have talked about the fact that Andrew, back in his residential setting was still not able to grieve about the loss of his grandmother or brother. I do remember several meetings between Charlie, Andrew, his therapist, and me when we talked with Andrew and tried to help him understand. In time, he would grieve in his own way, but not that summer.

As summer drew to a close, I knew I had to make decisions about seminary. I had only a few courses to finish my divinity degree, but I wondered if I could go on. Did I have the emotional fortitude to continue to study and pursue a career in ministry?

And then I began finding feathers.

I do not remember when the feathers first appeared. Perhaps it was about then. Often when I thought about the past or felt depressed, I discovered a feather in front of me—sometimes when I was in the yard but often in the house. At first, I told myself there was a totally logical explanation. Of course, birds lived near the yard or at the beach or in other outside places where I ventured. Still, the feathers always appeared right in my path, often when I was thinking of Jamie or looking for solace or direction.

On one hot August day as I mounted the stairs to the counseling office where I had seen clients for the past ten years, I reread the letter announcing the deadline for registration for seminary's fall semester at the end of the week.

What should I do? I wondered, agonized by the decision I must make.

As I fit the key into the lock of my office, I happened to glance down, and there on the carpeted floor was a feather with no apparent explanation for how it might have appeared there. Suddenly I remembered how proud Jamie had been when I enrolled in seminary. More taken with earth-based religions than traditional mainline denominations, Jamie was quite spiritual. He delighted in discussing his view of faith and how it compared to mine. Yes, I realized, Jamie would want me to go on.

"Okay, Jamie," I said picking up the feather. "I got it."

Despite my resolution to return to seminary, doing so presented quite a challenge. I had little energy and remained deeply depressed. I had shut myself off from all but the absolutely necessary. I hardly spoke to Jim, who said little about my inattention. I had only enough in my reserves to put one foot in front of the other doing what I had to do—the necessary acts of living each day, going to classes, and seeing the few clients I still had. All that felt like a full-time job and exhausted me.

My commute to seminary near Boston for classes gave me time to be alone and think. I mulled over the spring that had been the worst of my life and the summer that followed. I wondered if I would ever feel whole again. I did find some comfort in my seminary classes, although now I cannot even remember what I was taking. I recall several professors who—knowing what had happened in my life—were kind and understanding. They offered me leeway in completing assignments, but I determined to complete my work on time.

Chay and Becky had asked me to officiate at their wedding in September. Despite my grief and the lingering sorrow we all felt, I remember the wedding as a wonderfully festive event. Our two remaining children, their dad, his current lady friend, my husband, and I could together enjoy a ritual of continuing life. But once the festivities ended, I fell back into my depression that absorbed me like quick sand.

As fall dragged slowly on, the holidays loomed like gigantic black clouds on the horizon. Thanksgiving was a solemn affair with only our ninety-five-year-old friend, Myra, who spent holidays with Jim and me. I must have made the traditional Thanksgiving feast of turkey as was our custom, but I remember little of the meal or the day. Andrew spent the day with his father, and Chay, with his new in-laws. Maybe my children preferred others to my company right then, and that would be no surprise.

I had no desire to decorate for Christmas until a friend mentioned that, after her husband died, she made the first Christmas tree a memorial. That idea appealed to me. Abandoning familiar ornaments we had used for years, I began to search for ornaments that reminded me of Jamie or my mom. Encouraged by my seeming interest in something, finally, some friends gave me memory ornaments. I decked the tree with decorations depicting wolves, footballs and football players, dogs, and other animals to remember Jamie. For mom, I hung a violin (which she played), birds, a miniature teacup in honor of our chats over tea, and flowers.

The holiday took on new meaning. In the weeks before Christmas, I searched in shops for special ornaments that would remind me of the two people I had loved and lost. As Christmas approached I especially missed Jamie who had transformed into a child again at the mere mention of Christmas, but I found joy in the memorial tree.

Christmas was quiet and lonely without Jamie and Mom. Jim and I opened our presents Christmas morning. We invited our friend Myra to join us for dinner. But on that cold, bitter day, she said she would rather be home. Later, Jim and I took her a plate of Christmas dinner and found her bundled in the fleece blanket I had given her the past Christmas, sitting in her old chair and looking as dreary as we felt. She reminded me sadly of how it had been just a year ago when Jamie, the girl, Jim, Andrew, Myra, and I had shared Christmas dinner together, laughing and joking and consumed by merriment of the day. How much had changed in just one year.

"But we can't change it," Myra commented as she often did in her matter-of-fact Yankee manner. "We just go on." And so we did.

"Let's go up to Vermont for New Year's," Jim suggested the day after Christmas, no doubt hoping it would bring us both some pleasure.

I must have decided to take down the tree before we left. I am not sure why, as I usually left the tree up until January 6, or Little Christmas. Perhaps it had lost too many needles and we thought we should take it down rather than risking a fire hazard. As I put away the last memorial ornament, my energy drained again. There before me stood the unadorned tree, worn and largely denuded of needles. I felt as if I were looking into a mirror. I wondered if anything would ever feel right again.

Jim and I left for Vermont several days before the New Year. I remember little about the trip except that we visited our usual spots in southern Vermont. We probably spent a quiet New Year's Eve in our favorite bed and breakfast. The other days would have been taken up with sightseeing and visiting gift shops and scenic spots. But I remember little. I know that I spoke little, so enmeshed was I in my web of depression. As we drove home, I gazed out the window at light snow falling silently over icy fields. What a cold world, I thought. Cold and barren.

Jim stopped the car abruptly on the side of the road and jolted me from my thoughts.

"I can't do this any more!" he exclaimed, sounding tired.

"Do what?" I asked.

"Live with a ghost, a shell of the person who was my wife. I loved Jamie, too, but life goes on, and we need to go on too." Anger tinged his voice, and at first I responded with angry thoughts. How dare he! Looking back, maybe anger did me good as the first hint of emotion instead of sadness and depression. But no sooner had anger emerged briefly than I began to feel incredible fear. What if I lost Jim, too? Despite the fact that I had shut him out of my grief, he had been a rock—always there.

I began to cry, deep sobs that came from my depths, a torrent of all the emotion I had suppressed for months. I felt Jim's arms around me and knew I had to find a way to cope. I could not let myself slip deeper and deeper into depression lest I lose myself altogether and my husband as well. I resolved I would find a way to turn my life around.

I cannot say that it was easy to pull myself out of the depth of despondency. Depression required no effort. I need only exist. But I had to find resilience inside myself. How had I gotten through other difficult events in my life? What about the near death and frequent illness of my youngest son, Andrew, for example? Or the divorce that caused all of us such pain?

And then I remembered Jamie once telling me how he admired my fortitude.

"I'd like to be like you, Mom," he told me. "You always hang in there. I know that no matter how tough things get, we can count on you to be strong and get us through it." Where was the strength my son had so admired?

Soon after we returned from that trip, I had a terrible nightmare. In it, I relived the events of that horrible morning when we learned Jamie had died. I awoke sobbing, afraid it was happening again. Knowing Jim had already left for work and I was alone, I lay trying to erase the dream from my memory. But memories seemed to choke me. I could not face them. I was Mama Bear desperate to protect my cub from the consequences of being cast as the evil antagonist in a drama of love and potential murder. I could not make sense of the disconnect between events of that day, bits I had heard of how the media portrayed him, and what I knew of my son.

But I did know I had to face realities—at least some of them. With effort, I made myself place the memories in a chronological framework.

There was that Friday night when Jamie came home very upset.

"She took out a restraining order against me," he told me angrily.

"Gwen? For what?" I asked incredulously.

"She claims I tried to start a fire in the trunk of her car."

Ah, the car again. When Gwen came to live with us, it was obvious that she needed a way to get around and look for employment. Jim and I found her an inexpensive second-hand car, and I paid for it with the agreement that she would pay me back when she got a job. Once she moved out, it was clear I would never again see the car or what I paid for it. Jamie was angry about the situation.

"I cannot believe she would do that," he told me. "Just take off and not pay you for the car."

By then, I wanted it all behind me, and if that was what it took, I would write off the car as a bad debt. Although I knew Jamie was angry about the car, I doubted he would go do anything about it. I wondered if I was wrong about that.

Jamie told me he had a court date for the restraining order. Believing that the court would hear other accusations Gwen had made and recognize where the problem really lay, I assured him I would go with him. Perhaps Jamie was still concerned about the outcome of this complaint, but he seemed reassured. And then there was the note left for me on the table the next morning.

> Dear Mom,
>
> The wolf cannot be caged. Whatever happens, I will always love you.
>
> Child of your heart,
> Jamie

I remember thinking that the note was strange, but I did not see it as a final goodbye. That Friday evening, Jamie and I had a wonderful talk discussing his plans for the future; he seemed to have found a direction for his life. He told me he wanted to go back to college and had just completed his application.

Living with some friends with whom he went to high school, Jamie had started college the previous fall. But he soon realized that his time in the military had matured him in ways that made it difficult for his friends to understand.

"There's more to life than partying and fooling around," he told me. But it was the pressure Gwen put on him that was most difficult. Living with us, she begged him to come home from college every weekend. When he did, she gave him no time to study and expected him to spend all of his time with her.

"I can't do it and still stay up with my classes," he told me.

"Then stay at school and study. Don't give in to her," I counseled. But I knew the difficulty involved more than the conflict between

Gwen and college. I could see Jamie and the girl growing apart. The more they grew apart, the more she seemed to demand of him.

As the semester went on Jamie—torn between home with Gwen's ineluctable presence and school—showed the strain. His grades plummeted, and when the semester ended, it was clear that Jamie would not return to college.

We celebrated Christmas, and the holidays seemed to give all of us a respite from the tension developing in the house. I convinced myself that things would get better and threw myself into having Jamie home for the first Christmas in some years. We gave joyfully extravagant gifts as we gathered around the cheerfully lit tree—a mirage of happy family hiding festering disorder.

With childlike enthusiasm that made me wonder if her previous Christmases had been as full, Gwen merrily opened the gifts we gave her. The presence of my family and even the presence of this confused young girl warmed me. Did I have any idea that she would be not only surrogate daughter but the root of our undoing? I don't know. But as I watched the assembled family, I could almost recapture happy times when my children were small and their worries were, too.

As the holidays departed at the end of 2002 with a breath of cold New England winter air, so did our happiness. Jamie dropped out of school and lived at home with the intention of finding a job until he knew what he wanted to do next. His attitude toward Gwen fluctuated between polite distance and small instances of intimacies they had once constantly enjoyed. They had separate rooms. She responded from day to day with light coquettishness alternating with anger and accusations. Slowly, her neediness won out, and her volatility and moodiness made life difficult for everyone in the house.

Screaming at him hysterically while he tried to explain calmly or diffuse her anger, Gwen often lashed out at Jamie. I tried to stay out of their personal squabbles, but it became more and more difficult while living in the same house. Sometimes, the girl tried to triangle me into the argument.

"He's stolen my car keys!" She directed the accusation to me like a kindergärtner tattling on a peer. Jamie and I had been talking in the kitchen when she stormed in with this announcement.

"They are probably in your purse," he commented almost as an aside. In a few minutes, I heard the jingle of keys and the slam of the front door announcing her exit.

"In her purse," Jamie and I chimed in together in unified response. Despite our shared derision, I was concerned about the apparent escalation in Gwen's reactions to Jamie.

On another occasion, I came down the stairs to witness Gwen striking my son forcefully with her fists. He did not retaliate but tried to grab her arms to stem further assaults. When she saw me, the girl backed off, whirled, and dashed past me up the stairs to her room. Jamie appeared calmer than I would have expected.

"Does this happen often?" I queried. He shrugged and went into the kitchen to make himself a sandwich while I thought that we could not continue to live like that!

It seemed clear that something had ended the romantic relationship between Jamie and Gwen. Searching for solutions to our disrupted domestic life, I asked Jamie about their relationship as he and I sat together in the family room one evening. Gwen was not at home.

"I still care about her," Jamie told me, "but I now believe what my friends told me when we first started dating. She's not good for me. We come from different worlds."

Although I wanted to pursue his comment, I had more immediate concerns.

"Then we should ask her to leave," I told him. "We can't live like this."

"We can't ask her to leave until she finds a job and an apartment of her own," Jamie replied. "She is hundreds of miles from where she grew up. I brought her here. It wouldn't be fair just to kick her out."

"But I worry about you, Jamie," I told him. "What can I do to help?"

"Nothing, Mom. It will all work out."

As Jamie worried about whether he had done a disservice to Gwen by agreeing with me to bring her to live in our home hundreds of miles from anything familiar to her, she grew ever more demanding. Tension grew and I thought guiltily of my own part in this drama of unhappiness. As I look back—even now—I try to make sense of my feelings.

Why had I not seen that this girl needed to leave much earlier? True, Jamie felt it unfair to ask her to go, but perhaps if I had pointed out how unbearable it had become to live as we were, he may have recognized—as I did on some level—that for all of our sakes, she needed to go. Was there more preventing me from asking her to leave?

I thought of the day when Gwen first came to live with us. Remembering our meeting when I visited Jamie in Kansas, I looked forward to her arrival. She was warm, funny, and ingratiating. Looking back, I wonder if she revealed her authentic self. Had she with some keen sense recognized what I had longed for—a daughter with whom I could have a wonderfully close relationship like I had with my own mother. Was she longing for such a bond, too—one she reported never having with her own mother? Or did she only mirror my affection in an effort to bask in the comfort that we offered to her? I will never know.

Those first months after Gwen came, when she and Jamie were still undeniably a couple, were filled with laughter and companionship. I was the mother and loving the role. She asked for advice, and showed her new purchases. She seemed to see me as the person integral to her future. We cooked together, shopped together, and giggled together like sisters. Her slight, charming irreverence made me feel young. When she was not with Jamie, she was with me, sharing my life as I imagined a daughter would. I chalked off my mother's discomfort with her to jealousy at the closeness of our relationship. Looking back, I realize that everyone else perceived what I did not: that my view of the girl was too good to be true.

I had grown to love Gwen—my surrogate daughter, but I also saw what she was doing to my son. Should I have insisted earlier that she leave? Should I never have invited her? Had I contributed to my son's unhappiness because of my own needs? We struggled with our internal dilemmas, and life nonetheless went on.

Then came the letter from the Army. Although he had chosen to do the remainder of his tour of duty in the reserves, we all knew that Jamie could be called back to active duty any time. In March of 2003, President George W. Bush announced that the United States had begun military action against Iraq. Perhaps in anticipation of the event, Jamie received notice in mid-January.

He came in clutching the letter one morning.

"I'm going to Iraq," he told me. Almost elated, he handed the paper to me.

"Get your affairs in order," the letter said. "You will be deploying to Iraq."

Jamie drew up a will and readied himself for deployment. I felt sick at heart. I dared not share my feeling lest it become too real— that if Jamie went to Iraq, he would not return. It haunted me, but I tried to put it out of my mind. Every mother feels that way when her son goes off to war, I told myself. Yet, although I felt uneasy and worried when he was in Bosnia, I did not have the same sickening feeling then that he would not return as I did now.

With his deployment imminent, Jamie could not look for long-term work. He signed on with a temporary employment agency that placed him in several manual labor jobs.

"It feels great to be working again!" he told me. Although he exercised regularly, Jamie missed the rigorous physical activity and outdoor life that he had had in the Army.

January turned to February and February to March, but still no definite orders.

Those winter months were difficult for all of us. Technically a reservist, Jamie received word of imminent deployment within a month or so and then got notification of deployment cancellation. The cycle repeated three times in five months and left us all on a roller coaster of emotions about the uncertainty of Jamie's future— and ours.

In the meantime, apparently making Jamie's life miserable, Gwen remained with us. He stayed out more and more—probably to avoid contact with her—and lapsed deeper into depression. He often slept during the day and stayed up at night, roaming the house like a caged animal. I had not myself considered that the wolf cannot be caged. I worried about him but did not know how to ease his pain. All I knew was that I missed his ready smile and cheerful manner. By April, the tension in the house was untenable. Gwen finally had a job, but she made no effort to find an apartment.

Jamie came to me one night saying, "Mom, either I am leaving or she needs to go. I can't handle it any longer."

Finally I knew that it was time for the girl to go. I should have asked her to leave when Jamie returned home from school and there was such animosity between them. But Jamie had said it was unfair to send Gwen away until she had a place to go. Finally hearing the urgency in my son's voice, I realized that she must leave.

"This is your home," I told him. "I will ask her to leave."

I spoke with her the next day. I don't think she was surprised. All of us knew how difficult living together had become. Gwen said little in response, and I could not tell what she planned to do. That night, she did not come back to the house. Her clothes and belongings stayed, but we had no idea where she was. After she had been gone for three days with no word, I was concerned. Yes, we wanted her to leave, but I did not want her to come to any harm. Jamie, too, worried that something may have happened to her. He was concerned about friends she had made and wondered that she may have gotten into some kind of trouble. Finally, on the fourth day of her absence, Gwen called to say she was at a friend's and wanted to come and get her things.

I had packed some of her clothes for her, perhaps still clinging to a time when I felt like she was a daughter. I was not able to be there when she proposed to come. I asked Gwen only not to come while Jamie was there and told her when that would be. Not only did I feel it would be difficult for them to be together, but I also worried about how she might behave toward him.

When I returned home, Jamie told me that Gwen had shown up when he was home despite being asked not to. I asked what had happened, and he told me that there was just an awkward silence as she gathered the remainder of her belongings and left our home for the last time with no explanation about where she had been and no word of thanks for the months she had been under our roof. Angry and sullen, she left behind her a trail of hurt and disappointment. I had honestly felt I was helping this young woman and now wondered if anyone could alter the course of her confused life. I also felt a sense of betrayal, although I admonished myself for being selfish. I had loved this girl. I hoped we would be the family she said she had never had, but we could not be. I wondered who had failed—me in my idealism that one can really alter the course of another's life or Gwen in her inability to benefit from well-meaning compassion.

I thought back on my career as a social worker and later as a therapist. Over the years, I had learned that lives change only from within. How many times had I helped clients explore alternative ways of living only to have them sabotage their own efforts by returning to drugs, an abusive husband, or poor choices. As a therapist, I recognized that in the end one makes one's own destiny, whether filled with triumphs or heartaches. The realization made the sign I had affixed to my office wall even more telling: "The harvest of inner potential is the greatest gift that one can give to one's self".

By early May after Gwen left, things should have been better, but the possibility of deployment hung over Jamie's head. I suspected that he was eager to go and return to the squadron where he had been so involved. Gwen periodically phoned him on his cell. I am not sure what transpired or if they saw each other, but clearly Jamie was upset by the situation involving the girl.

He continued to suffer from symptoms that identify PTSD. His desire to isolate and not venture into crowds persisted along with his disrupted sleeping patterns and nightmares. I once found a scrap of paper—perhaps a diary page ripped out—where he wrote about his flashbacks of digging up dead bodies and fears of being blown up. It was an incredibly graphic and pain-filled writing that gave me chills. When I questioned him about it, he grabbed it from me, crumpled it, and cast it into the trash.

"Not your problem, Mom," he barked—and strode off.

As I look back, I wonder why, as a therapist, I did not recognize and perhaps even diagnose Jamie as having PTSD. Seeing him from the vantage point of mother blinded me to anything but his apparent pain.

Then came the announcement that Jamie would not deploy after all. After months of waiting for the proverbial other shoe to drop, the Army decided it didn't need him on active duty. I could feel Jamie's deep disappointment. I found it difficult to understand, since I felt relieved he would not have to venture again into danger.

No longer in limbo, Jamie found a job working with emotionally disturbed youth, a role that he looked forward to assuming. He reported that he enjoyed his first days at the job. Then came the Friday night he returned home and told me of the restraining order. By the time we finished talking that night, I believed things were looking up for my son. He no longer had to go into combat. I hoped that his troubles with his former girlfriend would soon resolve, even if it meant going to court.

How wrong I was.

A Cold Nose Warms the Heart

After Jim confronted me in Vermont, I thought that I owed it to him to face my grief and go on with my life. I should have recognized that I owed it to myself as well, but that was not my perspective. My resolve to put depression behind me and get on with living was not an easy prospect. Although I had returned to seminary classes at Andover Newton Theological School near Boston, my time at home often led to thinking, remembering, and grieving. While realizing that only I could pull myself out of depression, I tried to put on a guise of cheerfulness around Jim, because I had promised him I would try not to slump back into depression. Still, my time alone during the day when he was working seemed filled with black clouds.

The therapist in me recognized that grief-related depression is not something that can be covered up by a cheerful demeanor even if one wants to make the effort. I had helped many clients cope with significant losses in their lives and assured them that healing is a process—one that often takes as long as three years. I had seen others through the depression that often accompanies great loss. But now I was the one who felt mired in quicksand that would not release me. I could not imagine feeling that way for any amount time. Maybe the weight of the absorbing feelings would pull me totally under. In addition to recognition that I owed Jim more of a life than I could then give him, part of me determined to survive and find a way to emerge from the darkness.

There was so much I did not know. Perhaps in knowing more I would find answers and therefore some peace.

For one thing, I had many questions about what happened to Jamie. "Why?" became the overarching thought in my world. In addition, details of Jamie's death were hazy in my mind. I couldn't fathom that my son who had always seemed so full of life could end his life by his own hand in such circumstances.

Right after Jamie died, there were so many theories about what had happened. I had decided that, for the police, it was all cut and dried in a usual seemingly factual way. They provided an eager, statewide media with the titillating story that Jamie had broken into the house where Gwen was sleeping with her new boyfriend, wounded him, and killed himself. Although my friends and family insisted that I not read media reports, they told me that the reports differed depending upon the source.

I learned that some media reports quoted Gwen saying she believed Jamie wanted to kill her. I felt reporters tried to outdo one another in their sensationalism. After all, a shooting in a small town made big news. But police and media versions did not compute with me for several reasons. First, Jamie, an excellent marksman in the military, had dreaded the possibility of ever having to use his weapon against another human being. I could not imagine him intentionally setting out to kill or even harm anyone except a sworn enemy of the state whose military he served. I wondered about the more plausible suggestion involving Jamie and the other man struggling over the gun.

Then there was the talk that Jamie and I had the Friday before his death. He spoke of his concern about the girl and told me that he suspected that she was "going down the wrong path." He worried about the company she kept and where it would lead her. He obviously still cared about her, but it seemed more like the love of a brother than someone who had a romantic attachment to her. He seemed sincerely interested in her wellbeing despite his concern over the restraining order she had taken against him—an act that he said he honestly did not understand. The day he died, had Jamie gone to the house where the girl was not to harm her but instead with some misguided desire to save her from something?

I turned such thoughts over in my mind again and again. Desperate for answers, I decided to research the events of that night. My family had kept me from seeing newspaper reports or hearing anything on the radio or television, but the story was big news. It must have been difficult for them to keep me protected. On the Sunday we learned of Jamie's death, reporters camped outside our house. They came to the door several times, but concerned family and friends sent them away. We did not want to share our perspective on Jamie's death with the world, especially since we ourselves did not understand anything about it .

I thought of the day after Jamie's death when his dad, Charlie, and I went to tell our youngest son Andrew what had happened. We learned that the staff of the residential treatment center where he resided had tried to keep him away from any TV until we got there. But despite their best efforts, Andrew had heard whispering of staff and anxiously expected the worst.

During the weeks after Jamie's death, I got small pieces of the story. A friend told me that the media had called it a love triangle. That seemed absurd, given Jamie's feelings about Gwen at that time. Yes, it had been a big news story, but ironically, as I looked back and tried to understand, it seemed like I really did not know what happened.

In the weeks after Jamie's death, I went to the police station in the small town where Jamie died and talked with the charge officer assigned to the case. Obviously trying to understand what I was going through, he was caring and compassionate. He had talked with Jamie when Gwen took out the restraining order and commented, "I could tell your son was a nice guy." He seemed as puzzled as I was about what caused events surrounding Jamie's death.

I asked what had happened to Jamie's possessions in his truck when he died. The kindly town officer suggested that the state trooper might know. The state police trooper greeted my phone call with the same curtness he had shown us right after Jamie's death. He appeared suspicious of my desire to know what had happened and did not help my already precarious emotional state. In his mind, apparently, the reports in the media represented the facts of the situation. Case closed! End of discussion!

Later, I requested police reports, the autopsy, and anything I could get that would tell me what had happened. When they arrived months later, I couldn't look at them. I glanced at them quickly and saw that my son had died of a gunshot wound to the head and that there was no alcohol or drugs in his body. Then I put the reports away. It was too painful to read more. Although I still wanted to know what had actually happened, I knew that I could not fully face the reality. Instead, I would find ways to heal from the events that had permanently left a hole in my heart.

In early 2004, I tried to finish seminary classes. I expected perhaps that some material in courses would help me heal, as I anticipated helping others in the future. Perhaps it was the courses I took that semester—the final theoretical pieces I needed to complete my degree, but I found nothing of solace there other than the act of keeping busy. My therapist persona urged me to search for ways to fill my life with activities that would bring me pleasure, but I had difficulty finding any in those early days of healing.

I almost wished I still had the crazy schedule of teaching full time on top of going to seminary before Jamie died. At least then I would not have had time to think.

Sometimes, I gave Reverend Lois help when she needed an extra ministerial hand. It provided me with excellent practice at being a minister in a small church, my eventual goal. Reverend Lois made a superb mentor. She had had three students before me, all of whom kept in touch with her. I had met them all and found their occasional presence at church enjoyable. Their experiences as students in that small community church had been as rewarding as mine, and they, too, valued the Reverend Lois's tutelage.

I happened to see a notice at seminary calling for nominations for an award for excellence in field supervision. Aha! I thought. What a wonderful way to thank Reverend Lois for the time and care she had given all of us. I quickly contacted fellow former students whom Reverend Lois had supervised. We agreed that I would nominate Lois and they would support the nomination.

We were thrilled when we received word that Reverend Lois had won the award and would be honored at a presentation at Andover Newton. The event brought Linda, Patty, Ginny, Reverend Lois, and me together, piled into a multi-seated van to travel the seventy-five miles to Boston to support our mentor as she received her award. We had one more passenger. As Ginny Evans climbed into the van, she boosted up before her a medium-sized, gray Schnauzer who sat primly on the seat with the assurance that that was where he belonged.

"This is Lynks," Ginny introduced us all. The black eyes surveyed us knowingly and Lynks, finished with being introduced, curled into a ball where he would remain for most of our trip. I noticed that he sported an attractive red vest with the words "assistance dog" along with a logo that read "NEADS."

"What does NEADS stand for?" someone asked, admiring the appealing little dog.

Ginny explained that NEADS is an organization in Princeton, Massachusetts, that trains service dogs for people with disabilities as well as with people in helping professions. I had heard from Reverend Lois that Ginny had gotten a service dog for ministry, and the reality of a canine helper intrigued me.

"How do you use him?" I asked.

"He goes everywhere with me," Ginny explained. "On house calls, to hospitals and meetings. And he accompanies me in the pulpit on Sunday mornings."

I was fascinated and spent the entire drive to Boston quizzing Ginny about her service dog. She told me that Lynks was one of the first to assume the role as a ministry dog. NEADS places most dogs with people who have physical disabilities or hearing impairment. NEADS places a few dogs with helping professionals like therapists or teachers or, more recently, ministers. Chosen dogs are often especially friendly and suited to interacting with groups instead of one individual.

"It is amazing having a service dog for ministry," Ginny told me. "It brings a whole new dimension to my work. It is a wonderful icebreaker on Sunday morning. And dogs can be so soothing to those who are ill." She did not need to say any more. I was hooked.

The day after meeting Lynks, I called NEADS. I explained I was in seminary and wanted to apply for a service dog for ministry. To my disappointment, the very nice voice on the phone told me I had to be practicing as a minister before my application would be considered. Oh well, I thought. Someday.

For the next year, I threw myself into studies. Having come so far, I determined to finish seminary and find a church. I had another goal—to someday partner with a service dog for ministry.

It is amazing the momentum one can gain from intentionally trying to heal. Or was it the frenetic escape from the pain of grieving that spurred me on? In my therapy practice, I had often treated individuals who had recently lost a spouse. They found comfort in a frenzy of new activities, new friends, and new experiences. I often found that they danced as fast as they could not to experience the intense pain their loss brought into their lives. One widower came into his counseling appointment looking terribly haggard. He had seemingly been doing well, but suddenly he looked much older.

"I've tired myself out," he told me. "I have had lots of new experiences, I have made friends, and I think I am doing great. But when I look in the mirror, I still see the same shell that my Agnes left behind." Only after that realization could he allow himself to grieve fully for his wife of so many years.

Part of me recognized that my frantic, busy schedule was my way of escaping the hard work I still needed to do by grieving and healing. I knew from therapy training how long it takes to grieve a significant death fully, but I found myself thinking I did not have time for all that. With depression apparently behind me, I just wanted to get on with life. Perhaps I feared that down times would leave space for reflection and that reflection would be too painful.

But Jamie apparently did not intend to let me forget him. He still left me feathers. In the strangest places at the strangest times, I would look down and see a feather—a reminder of his presence in my heart if not in my literal world. It was also the time of wolves. Close friends knew that Jamie's symbol had been the wolf, and they knew that the wolf had taken on intense meaning for me. They began to give me "wolf things." From pictures, calendars, ornaments, statues, and even a doorstop, friends presented me with wolf items. With each I remembered the young man who had cared so deeply for that animal.

My therapy practice continued in the same building in the center of town. My friend Ellen, a massage therapist, had her office next door. We often spent our lunch times together in my office munching on our take-out salads while we talked—often of Jamie. Ellen once brought me a small stuffed wolf toy that adorned the mantel in my office from then on. From the beautiful depiction of a wolf painted on a piece of material that hung on the back of my chair to wolf greeting cards that lined my desk, memories of Jamie surrounded me.

My son also remained very much in my mind as I heard from Ron and Amanda about how their children were growing. Little Madison had joined Taylor, Jamie's goddaughter, and her younger brother Austin, who would have been Jamie's godson. Being a godfather meant so much to Jamie that when he died, I asked Ron and Amanda if I could be honorary godparent in his stead. They agreed, and I continued in that role without having met the children until I traveled to Kansas to see Taylor graduate from high school. I felt that Jamie would want me to be there in his place. Ron and Amanda have not let their children forget their Uncle Jamie, as they called him, who meant so much to them and who had such an impact on their lives.

Because they served in the same unit, Ron had been on alert to go to Iraq with Jamie before his death. Ron deployed the September after Jamie died. He told of a day in Iraq—November 2, 2003—that he felt changed his life.

Ron and his fellow soldiers had been told that they were going out on what was called a quick reaction force mission to help another military unit that had run into difficulty. Heading for the town of Al-Khaldiya, the soldiers prepared to leave camp while the mixture of heat and wind were, in Ron's letter to Jamie's brother Andrew years later, like "someone was blowing me in the face with a hair dryer." The soldiers donned their protective gear, grabbed their weapons, and loaded into their Bradley fighting vehicles. As a gunner in the Bradley, Ron sat alert in the turret scanning back and forth for a potential enemy strike. He explains:

I was especially looking for signs of an improvised explosive device. It may be at a disturbed spot on the side of the road or possibly a wire leading from a pile of rocks on the side of the road into the tall grass in the ditch. I knew it was my responsibility to ensure the road was clear because there was another Bradley behind us. I could feel the wind blowing the sand down into my gunner's hatch, like being hit by a sand blaster. The sand stuck to my sweat-caked clothes. It managed to make its way into every crack and crevice of my body. I knew that in about forty minutes I would be able to take off this gear that felt like it had doubled in weight since we left our camp. I just needed to stay focused and keep a sharp eye out for the "snake in the weeds."

Suddenly a flash burst that looked like the greatest fireworks display Ron and his fellow soldiers had ever witnessed followed by a bang "louder than thunder in a spring storm."

Ron's letter continues:

My head was violently slammed backward into the radios mounted directly behind my head. I attempted to re-open my eyes, but they felt as though someone stuck a hot poker in them. There was a strong smell of burnt hair, flesh, and gunpowder. I got my bearings back and called to my driver over the headsets as our vehicle stopped moving. I yelled, "Are you okay?"

He responded, "Yes. What the hell was that?"

I told him that I had no idea.

I looked to my right, and my Bradley commander was pale in the face and looked as though he was about to throw up. He looked into my eyes and said, "Whatever you do, don't let me die."

I looked down at his leg. It looked like it had been put through a meat grinder. I told him to put on a tourniquet and that he would be fine. What else could I do?

As I began to scan for the insurgents that had hit us, I felt a sense of calm spread throughout my body. I knew something wasn't right, but I wasn't sure what it was. I reached down and felt my right calf. There was a warm, wet spot as if someone had poured a bucket of warm water right onto my leg. Only it wasn't water that I felt. It was my own blood. But there was no time to worry about that because I had to get us back to our camp. As I continued to scan the road, I told my driver to get us back to camp as fast as possible.

Back at camp, Ron was rushed to the hospital. He thought of his wife and children and prayed that he could return to them. Although he would keep his badly injured leg, it would give him excruciating pain for years until it was eventually amputated. Nonetheless, he is convinced that his close friend Jamie was riding with that Bradley vehicle on that day. As Ron explains:

> I am thankful, for I truly feel on that second day of November in 2003 Jamie was my Guardian Angel. For if the round that struck our Bradley had gone just another inch, it would have passed through the vehicle creating a suction type affect like that described of black holes and would likely have killed all three of us that were in the vehicle. Jamie had left this legacy behind. But he was gone now, and I knew that all of our lives must go on.

It was comforting to think about what Jamie's life had meant to others, but I also knew it was time to work on my own life. As spring 2005 drew near, I realized that the graduation from seminary I had so diligently pursued was almost a reality.

And then it was the day. I can picture it—the day of culmination of years of study and a lifetime of expectations. With conflicting emotions swirling in my head, I am marching up the aisle of a stately old church. I feel emptiness at the absence of Jamie and my mother, two people to whom my graduation would have meant so much. Jim, Chay, and his wife, Becky, are all here, and I am warmed by their presence. As I sit among my classmates, I glance up at the huge stained glass window shedding light on all of us despite the cloudiness of a rainy afternoon. What a journey it has been. I think of how I had come to this day.

I envision my childhood when I watched my minister father as he conducted worship and thought I would like to do that someday.

In college, I studied religion, but women were not then often ordained. It was not an easy path.

And then life intervened as it so often does, for me in the form of a career in social work, a husband, and three fine children. Not until I found myself at the end of a twenty-five year marriage and feeling adrift did the ministry once more call to me.

My minister at the time, Reverend Natalie Maynard, asked if I had ever considered the ministry.

"A lifetime ago," I laughed. She suggested I attend a conference at Andover-Newton Theological School—a conference designed for those who wondered if they heard the call to ministry. "Sure. What could it hurt?" I thought.

I enjoyed a weekend with several dozen men and women who stayed on the campus and attended workshops designed to help each of us discern if we had a call to ministry. As the weekend ended, I began thinking about all I had to do with my children at home. My mom had watched them for the weekend, and I was anxious to get home. The last event was a chapel service, and I considered leaving early and not attending it. Then I checked myself. "You came to this! You might as well stay for the entire experience."

An old and picturesque stone structure with stained glass windows adorning the rear wall, the small chapel for closing worship nestled on the side of a hill. The sun gave off the last rays of brilliant reddish gold light near sunset on that February day. I took my place quietly with other worshipers. I felt keen awareness of the glorious light streaming through the windows. As we rose to sing a hymn, the light seemed to bathe me personally as the voices raised in song:

> Here I am, Lord. Is it I, Lord?
> I have heard you calling in the night.
> I will go, Lord, if you lead me.
> I will hold your people in my heart.

A feeling came over me like none I had ever experienced. I knew then that the ministry called.

And so, here I am at graduation after eight years of study punctuated by the deaths of two people I loved. But I have made it. I feel their presence as I emerge with my diploma into the bright sunlight. The rain has stopped.

Despite graduation and a feeling of accomplishment, I did not yet look for a church. Almost two years had passed since Jamie and Mom's death, but I still felt unprepared emotionally to minister to others. Reverend Lois graciously encouraged me as her informal assistant, and my healing heart found solace among the people of North Orange.

In the meantime, I decided to pursue another dream. As soon as I graduated from seminary, I sent my application to NEADS. By the end of May, they called me for an interview.

Talk about nervous.

The client coordinator, Kathy Foreman, invited me to the Princeton NEADS campus and greeted me warmly. We discussed my desire for a ministry dog, my life style, and my previous experience with dogs.

Dogs had been an integral part of my life from the little Cocker Spaniel who guarded my carriage when my mother took me to the corner store as an infant to the German Shepherds and Basenjis my parents raised as I grew up. We always had at least one dog. Sometimes to my mother's dismay, my father had a way of acquiring them. While I was away at college, Dad wrote me of the family who came to our house to buy one of our Shepherds. They brought with them a pathetically thin miniature poodle whose long hair was so matted and dirty that what my father assumed was a brown dog later turned out to be light gray. The little dog was so skittish that my father guessed it had been mistreated. The people themselves were course, rude, and impatient. There was no way that Dad intended to sell one of our dogs to them. He told them that all of the puppies were spoken for and then, eying the pathetic poodle, asked if they would sell him.

"Sure, he's a pain in the neck!" the man told him. They struck a deal for ten dollars. When my mother returned from work, she discovered that not only had my father not sold a puppy, but she and Dad had gained a scruffy little dog instead. Cleaned up, he was quite presentable. Showered with affection, he quickly grew to be a wonderful pet and got on famously with the much larger Shepherds.

The interview with Kathy went well, and at its completion, she ushered me upstairs to the training room to meet several dogs and Brian, the trainer who would assess my ability to work with them. I had assumed that a service dog would be a larger dog and had been surprised when Ginny's Lynks was a Schnauzer. I envisioned meeting Golden Retrievers or Labrador Retrievers and was not surprised when Brian brought out Betsy, a lovely ginger-colored Golden Retriever. She was friendly, obedient, and eager to please, which I later learned marks NEADS-trained dogs. I had an opportunity to put the dog through her paces. Then, as I handed her back to her trainer, Brian presented me with another.

"This is Dandi," he told me. "Let's see how he feels to you."

As I started off to work with the dog, I looked down—and down— to see beside me a small, grey bundle of exuberant fluff gazing up at me from under a lock of hair that almost covered his trusting black eyes. It had been a long time since I had worked with a dog so small. Granted, my parents had raised medium-sized Basenjis for a time, and I had shown them, but I was accustomed to big dogs. Shepherds counted as my ultimate favorite.

Instead, along beside me bounced a little fluff ball—a Shih Tzu, Brian told me—who was as enthusiastic, obedient, and energetic as the Golden had been. And beneath the flop of bangs, I saw a twinkle in those little eyes that won my heart.

Brian praised my abilities in working with the dogs and was not surprised that I had worked with dogs before. It soon became clear that NEADS had chosen Dandi for me.

Little did I know that the interview would significantly change my life.

New Windows, Opening Doors

Thrilled at the completion of my interview at NEADS, I learned I would attend a week of training in early September when Dandi would officially become my partner in ministry. In the meantime, I had a lot to do.

With the dog part of my life in place, I turned my thoughts to plans for the ministry. Just knowing I would not be alone in the venture gave me confidence. I decided I was ready to take the next step.

Before I could consider being ordained as a minister, I had to fulfill preliminary qualifications. First I must write an ordination paper, a lengthy document outlining my beliefs about faith and how I would interpret them to my future congregations. I would then present my faith statement and defend or explain what I had written before a gathering of fellow clergy and lay people called an ecclesiastical council. The council would vote to determine if I demonstrated sufficient preparation to pastor a church. From there, I would create a profile and send it to the national United Church of Christ office in Cleveland to circulate among churches seeking a pastor where I might be a good fit. Although some denominations allow ordination immediately after seminary, my own UCC, Congregational ordains only after one has received a call to a specific church. In other words, the job offer arrives before the ordination. Although I was not sure if I was ready for my own church, I decided nevertheless to have my ecclesiastical council while theoretical material from seminary was still fresh in my mind.

I would not have chosen to have my council on Father's Day, but I vied with other would-be ministers for dates, and that was the day assigned to me. Perhaps there was significance, too. After all hadn't my minister father influenced me in choosing the path toward ministry?

It is natural to be nervous when facing a group of one's peers ready to question you on the smallest detail of your theology and beliefs. I certainly felt nervous as I looked out on the sea of faces gathered at the Community Church on that Father's Day. My family was there to cheer me on, including Jim, who as a Roman Catholic all of his life had never been privy to such a process and maybe wondered how the Protestant way measures up.

The small church was full and the congregation ripe with anticipation as, according to custom, I read my ordination paper and awaited questions. The first few queries were fairly straightforward and easy, and I began to settle in. Then came the question from a woman whom I had come to know as the wife of one of my advisors. She knew my history well.

"How does your son's death inform your future ministry?"

As I drew a breath to compose my answer, I saw Jim's face, his jaw clenched in apparent anger. No doubt he felt the question inappropriate. But as I thought about it in those moments of preparation to respond, I felt the question quite appropriate and one I could comfortably answer.

"I believe my son's death has prepared me for ministry in a unique way," I began.

"It is not easy to lose a child," I continued.

> We never anticipate that our children will die before we do, and somehow it upsets the natural order of things. The experience altered the way that I look at a great many things. It gives me a perspective that only someone who has experienced the death of a child can fully understand. I believe it will help me minister to others—not only to help them with the death of loved ones but also to bring understanding and compassion to parents who have lost their own children.

As I uttered those words, I had no way of knowing that my future pastorate would bring me to a church where many people had lost children and that my own experience in losing Jamie would do much to guide me as I ministered to that congregation.

When I had answered all questions posed, the council sent me from the room, then deliberated and voted. As I returned, hearty applause and a standing ovation let me know I had successfully completed my oral exam and could look for a call from a church.

At home that evening, I was exhausted and glad to throw on a bathrobe and anticipate a quiet evening. As I started to change my clothes, the phone rang. Since the phone was at the top of the stairs, I grabbed it, wriggling into my robe.

"Is this the mother of James Tower?" a young male voice asked.

Sure that it was some telemarketer who did not realize that Jamie was gone, I irritably replied "Who is this?"

"You don't know me," the voice continued. "My name is Adam. I was in the Army with Jamie."

He had my attention. I sat on the stairs to listen.

"I have been feeling all day like Jamie wanted me to call you—like it was a special day. I know it's Father's Day, but I couldn't imagine that was the reason. I don't know. I just felt like he wanted me to call."

Tears sprang to my eyes as I told the young veteran it was a special day for me and why.

"I'm sure you did well," he told me. "The way Jamie talked about you—well, he thought you were really special." Clearly a young man who was not used to flowery speeches, he stammered.

"Thanks," I said. "I think Jamie was pretty special, too."

"That he was, Ma'am. I was so upset when I heard about his death, I mean." He stumbled self-consciously over his words. I wasn't sure what the fruit of the veteran grapevine had yielded, but I didn't want to go there right then. He must already know some version, as he did not press me for any details. Instead, he began to tell me about his Army life with my son, something that warmed my heart—the best gift that life could give me at that very moment.

Always interested in Jamie's friends, I listened appreciatively as Jamie's buddy told me about his life. It pleased me when he offered to email me a picture. We ended the long call with his promise to do just that.

"How strange," I thought, "that Adam should call at just this time when I was on an emotional high from having passed my ecclesiastical council." Then I smiled. Not so strange really.

"Thanks, Jamie, for having your friend convey your message of support."

Several days later, I checked e-mail at my therapy office and noticed an unfamiliar address. Opening it, I discovered it was Adam and expectantly opened the picture attachment. He sent a photo of a lovely water scene on a lake, perhaps, with a handsome young man standing in a small motorboat with his foot casually resting on the bow. He smiled out at me from the screen, and I could almost imagine Jamie calling to him from the dock and joking companionably.

I had told Jim about the phone call and was anxious to show him the picture. About to leave for the day, I hurriedly pushed "print" and started to get my books and papers together to take home. I grabbed the printed sheet from the printer, folded it, and stuffed it in my folder. I decided I would look at it when I got home. But when I got home, dinner preparations were foremost on my mind, and I did not think of the picture until later.

After doing the dishes, I sat at my computer to answer email and do a bit of work before I went to bed. I suddenly remembered the picture of Adam. I found the folded sheet in my papers and said to Jim, "Here, I want to show you something," handing it to him to unfold.

He scanned it and looked at me quizzically, "A boat?"

"Yes, but look at the young man in it. He knew Jamie in the Army." I moved in to look at the picture with him.

"I don't see . . . " Jim began. I took the paper from him. There was the lake scene with the lovely little boat just as I had seen it. But the boat was empty. It was as if the two young men calling to each other, one from shore and the other from the boat, were both gone and the lone boat stood as a testament to my own aloneness.

To this day I have no explanation for the picture. At first I tried to explain it away by thinking that the printer only printed part of the picture, but it was the same size picture that I had seen in my office. Jim said calmly, "Nice picture" and slowly walked away. Hastily I went to my computer and found the email gone, possibly inadvertently deleted by me.

But then a feeling of peace came over me, and I did not need to recreate the picture as I had originally seen it. It was enough for me that Adam had somehow been moved to call me on the day of my ecclesiastical council. I had no doubt who had been at work in giving me that gift. My son still looked out for me.

As summer went on I found myself more able to get back into writing. It was time to revise a college text I had written, probably a good way to get back into writing. Although time-consuming, revisions do not require the same concentration as the book I had to write from scratch. That book, the one due soon after Jamie's death, still sat on the back burner and would for some years—not due to my own ability to return to it but rather because of other more pressing projects required by my publishers.

For a few summer weeks, I returned to the cabin in the woods, the best place I have found to write. Sometimes Jim and I spent time there, and for a time my son Andrew joined me in our woods retreat. Since I had scattered Jamie's ashes there, I found myself warmed by his presence. I had no graveyard marker to decorate with flowers, but I had the beauty of the woods, the rushing of the brook, and the song of the birds as testament to my son's life. That was enough.

I spent Sundays helping Reverend Lois at the Community Church, glad to have the opportunity to preach once in awhile. I also started my ministry profile, an exhaustive document with my qualifications for ministry along with multiple recommendations I requested. Once finished, the profile would go out to churches seeking a pastor. Information in my profile would tell them if I might fit their needs. In turn, I would have an opportunity to see profiles of any churches that had an interest in hiring me.

My profile had to be done online and connected to the database at UCC headquarters in Cleveland. The online requirement carried the kinks of something new. That and my own limited skill on the computer meant I spent time and effort redoing parts of the profile as either the main data bank or I lost what I had done previously. It created a late summer of frustration, and I longed for September. I looked forward, too, to my new life with a service dog.

Back to writing and helping out at the church, I felt I was healing nicely, but at my core remained an emptiness—a void that I imagined would never be filled. I realized how long it takes to heal. Not that one ever forgets, but after three years, most people can go on and live full lives. I knew I wasn't "there" yet. Despite what I knew of the psychology of grief, I wondered if I ever would be. Ever praying that something would give me hope and wholeness once more, I busied myself with the tasks at hand.

The evening of Labor Day, I reported to NEADS for training with my new dog. NEADS has a lovely campus nestled in the woods of central Massachusetts. The campus then consisted of administration and training buildings and a comfortable five-bedroom cottage where clients stayed during their training period. The NEADS staff as well as two special education teachers, Tracy and Lori, and two women scheduled to receive dogs for the hearing-impaired greeted me. We each had a spacious bedroom with single bed and huge dog bed in one corner. First message: the dog sleeps in his or her bed, not yours. Message received. I remembered the size of Dandi, the dog intended for me. I decided I would have to search for him in the morning in a bed that large.

My eyes welled up as a memory pushed itself into my thoughts, a memory of Jamie as a toddler curled up asleep in the giant dog bed we had for our German Shepherd. How Jamie would have loved this place with its vague but not unpleasant smell of dog and its relaxed atmosphere. Yes, Jamie would have been quite at home here, and I had no doubt that he was with me in spirit.

My two special education colleagues, one from Rhode Island and the other from Washington State, were as excited as I was to be training with a dog. Their dogs would help with their students in the classroom. They were both fascinated that some dogs served for ministry, and as they asked questions, I realized that I, too, had a lot to learn about the duties of such a dog. We chatted companionably, and I found myself looking forward to the week ahead.

As we talked, the two women who would receive hearing dogs came in from the other side of the house. We introduced ourselves all around and began talking about why we wanted dogs. At least one of the women had been deaf from birth, and her speech revealed someone who had not been able to mimic sounds she heard. She read lips well, though, and we conversed easily. It moved me when she explained that she had a baby and her hearing impairment prevented her from hearing him cry.

My eyes filled with tears as she told her story. Her words and emotion took me back to the days when my own children were babies. I felt so protective of them. Each whimper had me at their sides trying to discern their needs. What if I could not have heard them cry? What if I had not known when to go to them? I teared up again as I listened to the young woman and blessed NEADS for giving her a hearing dog that could alert her to her baby's voice.

As we all talked, I marveled at the role of hearing dogs. The other women had apparently done their own homework well and knew some of what to expect. When a hearing dog hears a sound—a doorbell, the ring of a phone—it is trained to alert its human partner by going to him or her, sometimes nudging or even jumping up to let the person know there is a sound. For example, the doorbell rings. The dog looks to the sound, goes to its partner and back to the sound, beckoning the partner to come and attend to it. Dogs also learned to alert their partners when someone calls his or her name. In this case, the hearing dog would tell a young mother when her baby cried.

As I climbed into the comfortable bed at NEADS that night, I felt pleasantly exhausted by the wealth of information I had already taken in. Little did I imagine how tired I would be by the end of the training week.

The next day, after a few classes on how-tos, we met our dogs. Tracy received Betsy, the Golden Retriever I met when I attended my screening. Lori got a tiny Boston Terrier whose name, Genevieve, was longer than her whole body. I was not surprised when Lori was soon calling her Gen, which better fit her diminutive size. Only when scolded did Gen warrant a stern "Genevieve!" And here came Dandi, prancing out to meet me as if to say, "There you are! I thought we were going to be partners, and then you disappeared."

Maybe I just had a wishful voice in my head, but he did look pleased to see me. I was certainly thrilled to see him. Did he know, I wondered, that I was to be his new "forever person"? As he looked up at me, I believed he smiled. I would later learn that Shih Tzus like Dandi have a funny little parade rest stance when their bottom teeth stand out from their upper lips. Thus, the dog seems to smile.

Our trainer was Brian, whom I would come to respect and admire for his talent and compassion with dogs. As far as people, well. Initially Brian scared the heck out of me. Not that he was unkind or even gruff. But he has the same standards for the people he trains as he has for dogs. He expects that the people will be well-trained and good at what they do. Recognizing a master at his training art, I wanted to please him. I had worked with dogs. This shouldn't be that tough, right?

But I was accustomed to a dog with its head in easy reach of my hand at my side. And here I was with twelve pounds of exuberant fluff whose head didn't even reach my kneecap. Whenever I gave him a command, I felt inclined to bend over—perhaps to make sure that he could hear me way down there? Throughout the training, Brian barked a constant admonition to me: "Stand up straight!" I shot up straight at least until the next time I gave my dog a command. Nevertheless, with appreciation that we had been assigned to him, I loved Brian's way of training.

Our week consisted of learning the dogs' commands, practicing working with them both on campus and on trips to local stores like the supermarket or WalMart, and considering the finer points of caring for a service dog. After the first night, our dogs stayed in our individual rooms, thus helping us bond and get used to one another.

Our first night was a bit chillier than usual September weather. I snuggled under the warm comforter of my bed after giving my small dog a command to go to his bed. He eyed it speculatively. Perhaps he, too, wondered if he would get lost in its spacious folds. Cognizant perhaps of its previous occupants, he sniffed it, turned around a few times, and then popped back up to trot over to my bed and stare up at me. If you have ever looked into the warm brown pleading pools of a hopeful dog's eyes, you will know how difficult it was for me not to scoop him up on the bed with me.

"You are supposed to sleep over there!" I tried to sound like the alpha, but I do not think I fooled Dandi. Determined that I would play by the rules, I ordered him to his bed once again. We had a momentary standoff—quite unlike the previous behavior of the little dog who had obediently and without question done my every bidding throughout the past day. Until, with a huge sigh of resignation he found a place on the big dog bed and curled up to sleep. He probably figured, I mused, what a cold-hearted human he had gotten in the placement lottery.

The next morning it had warmed considerably, and the sun shone brightly through the windows. Dandi, still buried in his dog bed, opened one eye as I bounded out of bed eager to begin the day's activities. Reluctantly, he raised himself, yawned, and gave a big stretch, perhaps wondering why he couldn't sleep a bit longer. But when I snapped on his leash and suggested we go out, he forgot his weariness and, with characteristic enthusiasm, trotted along by my side.

We were apparently the first to rise, so we had the yard to ourselves. The expanse behind the guest house is wooded and serene. A very short walk takes one to a small pond with a bench on the shore. How tranquil, I thought, as Dandi did his morning doggie duties. It was just what I needed. We walked for a bit, and then I sat on the bench overlooking the pond. Its silvery scales reflecting in the morning sunlight, a fish jumped. Dandi looked at me quizzically, and I wondered what went on in his little brain. "Should I catch that?" "What is that thing?" But I had no way of knowing his thoughts, and he finally curled up in the sunshine at my feet.

After a quick breakfast, we resumed our classes. We saw little of the two women with hearing dogs, as they had a different trainer with different tasks and schedules. But Tracy, Lori, and I became close. As we learned together, it seemed that Dandi and little Gen, the Boston Terrier, had developed an infatuation with each other. Whenever we were idle, they somehow managed to lie as close to each as possible, often curled comfortably back-to-back. Fortunately, Gen's human partner, Lori, and I had become friendly, and so the budding canine romance blossomed. When we allowed the dogs to play off duty in the large training room or in the enclosed exercise yard, Gen and Dandi played together with the abandon of the young and—we humans decided—in love.

They had their devilish moments, too. One afternoon as we exercised in the fenced-in yard, the two women and I were in stitches as we watched the three dogs run, Dandi and Gen taking turns doing figure eights under the belly of the much larger Golden, Betsy, without ever breaking their stride. Betsy took it good-naturedly until they all became bored with the game and plunked down, tongues lolling in dog-tired pants.

At the end of the day, the training and challenges of it once more exhausted me. But I enjoyed the tiredness as I thought of my two new friends, Tracy and Lori, our meals together, and our conversations between classes. I realized that for the first time in quite a while, I felt at peace with myself. That night, as I listened to the soft snores of my little dog dutifully curled up in his own bed, I thought of what a balm the experience provided for my tired and wounded soul. I recognized I would rather be nowhere else on earth at that moment. I would look back on the week as one of the most wonderful of my life.

Another day of classes came and went. Dandi and I became more of a team. Tracy, Lori, and I marveled at how good we felt and at the rejuvenating experience it was. The atmosphere impressed us all—a warm, homey feeling where everyone seemed to know her or his job, enjoy it, and work well with others. One day after classes, the then-NEADS director Sheila O'Brien called to us from the doorway. "May I come in?" she asked.

We greeted her warmly and shared our wine. I would learn to care a great deal for Sheila as time went on and to admire all she had done to develop the wonderful program at NEADS.

The week of training ended too soon, although I longed to get Dandi home and introduce him to Jim. I wondered if I was ready to leave the sheltering safety of the training setting. I hated letting go of the experience.

When Lori, Tracy, and I finally bade farewell, we promised to keep in touch. We allowed Gen and Dandi a good-bye snuggle before we went our separate ways. As I drove out of the driveway on that Friday afternoon with many warm thoughts and memories, I experienced some trepidation. Would I keep up Dandi's training?

I heard Dandi move in his crate in the seat behind me and felt comforted. I couldn't wait to begin our life together and wondered where the path would lead us.

Building Hope

When we arrived home from training, Jim greeted us as he perhaps wondered what life would be like with this new animal. But it was not long before Dandi had clearly won his heart.

When we met, Jim had been grieving the loss of Jack and Mitchell, his two large dogs who remained with his ex-wife when he moved to an apartment. He especially missed Jack, a part Lab and part Saint Bernard, his constant companion and from Jim's description more the size of a horse than a dog. Jim frequently recounted their adventures with obvious longing. I wondered how Jim would feel about a twelve-pound Shih Tzu, but from the moment we arrived home from training, he took to Dandi. Dandi, although bonded to me as his primary human, soon gave Jim the okay in his book. He considered Jim the go-to person if I were not around. He even got used to being called Larry, Jim's affectionate name for him.

Jim loves to give people nicknames, and the nickname sometimes overtakes the person's actual name in our conversations. Jim has a friend actually named Larry, a short, stocky individual who sports a bushy grey beard and longish hair. Jim decided that Dandi reminds him of his friend and promptly started calling my new dog Larry. To my surprise, after an initial hesitation, Dandi answered to the name when Jim called him by it, and he always responds to either Larry or his own name.

I wondered how Dandi would do with our four cats. I had two cats, and when my mother came to live with us during the last week of her life, her cats came, too. Although I thought I would find homes for them after Mom died, I could not bring myself to do it. So Ebony and Monty joined our household with my own cats, Bootsie, a huge tuxedo cat who ruled the household, and Snowflake, a diminutive pure white and tiny part Manx. Snowflake distinguished herself by leaping onto tall counters in a single bound, a skill I did not appreciate.

Dandi developed a different relationship with each cat. In training, he and the other dogs had been exposed to cats. When he first arrived at our house, he barely took notice of his new feline siblings.

But the cats noticed him. Intent upon letting him know that this was her house and she would not tolerate any interloper who expected to challenge her authority, Bootsie stood her ground. Dandi silently and gracefully agreed to her terms, thus insuring their future harmony. Ebony, a sweet cat, took Dandi's presence in his stride. Snowflake, who runs from everyone and everything, ran from Dandi. Dandi decided that it was a game and ran after her, which frightened Snow. Snow and Dandi eventually developed a truce with them lying back to back on my bed while ignoring each other.

Monty, the smaller black and white cat, really took to Dandi. They became fast friends. Partially blind from an accident when he was a kitten, Monty probably needed a friend. The other cats tolerated him, but from the moment he arrived, Dandi treated Monty as something special. They often lay curled up together. When Dandi returned from being out with me, Monty greeted him and rubbed against him as if to say 'Where've you been? I'm glad you're back!".

As I watched my perky little dog adjust to his new home, acclimating to the cats and staking out his own territory, I wondered what Jamie would have thought of him. Often when I thought of Jamie, I heard his voice in my head commenting as he might have commented in life. Now I could hear him chuckling and saying, "*That's* a dog?" Jamie, too, was fond of large dogs like our German Shepherd mixes. He would have chuckled at mom's lap dog. Ironically, Dandi decidedly does not choose lap dog status—his choice. He stands up to anything—except balloons popping. In spite of his size, I knew Dandi would win Jamie over as he had won us all over.

A new service dog requires plenty of attention. The biggest adjustment perhaps involves the need to plan. You have to remember that you have a dog that goes with you everywhere and make accommodations for him. I needed to remember his service dog cape, extra water for him to drink, a dish, his leash, and anything else required.

I learned that Dandi found ways to be needed. When I do the laundry, I prefer to bring the dried clothes up into the den to fold rather than folding them in the musty cellar near the washer and dryer. One evening I folded clothes, and Dandi reached into the basket and brought me a sock. I chuckled and exchanged it for a treat.

"Too bad you can't get the other one!" I laughed, ruffling his furry head. Immediately he dug in the basket for another sock and brought it to me. Amazingly, he found the mate to the first sock. Dogs are supposed to be color blind, but Dandi easily discerns the difference between the white crew socks I wear with jeans and Jim's darker grey work socks. We fold laundry together, and he always brings me the correct mate. People have told me that it is not possible until I demonstrate Dandi's abilities. Someone from NEADS later explained that it was Dandi's keen nose and ability to detect my scent from Jim's that was responsible for his choosing the correct socks—rather than his ability to discern color. But I was still impressed.

I soon learned that Dandi loves to fetch things. All service dogs learn to fetch objects like keys and portable phones to help their human partners. Even ministry and therapy dogs learn such skills as they were initially trained as service dogs. Dandi took his lessons seriously. In fact, I often had to remind him to wait to be asked to fetch objects. Otherwise, he liked to collect anything within reach and bring it to me: a great house-cleaning tool, but not necessarily a safe practice for my small dog who might pick up something he should not have.

Dandi's engaging personality, his attention to me, and his desire to please boosted my spirits. I noticed how much better I felt. No longer did days drag on. Rather, each day filled with new experiences. My pint-sized pup gave me a purpose and someone always at my side bringing joy. I began to feel myself healing. Life seemed brighter, and the future filled with hope. There was also something comforting about Dandi's warm presence. His total focus on me gave me confidence that he was always on hand when I felt the need of comfort.

As a service dog for ministry, Dandi had another role to play as my helper. I created a letter for area churches and organizations offering to talk about Dandi as a service dog for ministry. Several organizations asked us to speak and delighted in Dandi's antics. After my presentation, I would ask Dandi to tug open a small plastic drawer. Dandi enjoyed the demonstration so much that he would often go to the little plastic chest to perform his task as soon as I began to speak.

I also kept busy by helping out at the Community Church after Reverend Lois retired. I preached at several other churches doing a Sunday here and there as a supply pastor. Dandi always accompanied me, and church members greeted him enthusiastically.

During the summer of 2006, I accepted a temporary preaching role for some weeks at a church whose pastor was on sabbatical. The Trinitarian Church in Warwick, a small but active church, meets in a building that looks more like a house than a church. There, I found a warm and friendly congregation. Dandi, always ready for a new group of adoring folks, greeted everyone with equal enthusiasm, and he was a special favorite with the congregation's children.

My extended duties in Warwick gave me a taste for a church of my own. As I healed from losing Jamie and my mother, I itched to try my skills as pastor of my own church. I dusted off my profile and started to look at churches in search of a minister.

A visit to an orthopedic surgeon interrupted my quest when I learned that my right knee joint had so little cushioning material that bone rubbed against bone. I needed a total knee replacement. At first petrified by the prospect, I talked with Reverend Lois, who herself had recently had the procedure. Almost into the holiday season, I made arrangements for the surgery in mid January of the following year.

As I thought about having surgery, I worried about what I would do with Dandi. After the anticipated week-long hospital stay, I preferred to go home rather than to rehab. The thought of being away from home, Jim, and Dandi did not seem conducive to healing. Fortunately, a couple of friends and neighbors agreed to help care for Dandi while Jim worked during the day. My pint-sized companion turned out more of a blessing than a concern.

Surgery went well, and despite intense pain, I looked forward to getting home. Not able to tolerate medications prescribed for pain, I had a difficult first few days at home. Pain tends to block out other sensations, but I do remember the worried face of Dandi gazing up at me as I reclined on the couch during the day, trying desperately to find a comfortable position. As I felt better, I took more notice of Dandi and his activities.

Dandi took the days of my recovery in stride, often trying to assist me in a variety of ways. After descending the stairs using different—often not too graceful—methods suggested by the physical therapist, I hobbled with a walker to get breakfast. Using the walker's basket, I carried my portable meal and installed myself on the couch to await whoever had agreed to walk Dandi, the physical therapist, and friends who might drop in. As Dandi watched the process, I wondered if he was thinking about how he could possibly be helpful. Perhaps he decided that it was enough not to get in my way.

Once I was on the couch, Dandi was as attentive as any mother hen. If my blanket slipped off onto the floor, he would be at my side, one corner in his mouth to help me to pull it back on. When the remote for the TV sat on another table, he joyfully brought it to me. Once I left the portable phone on a chair out of my reach. Before I had a chance to ask for it, I heard a clunk as the phone hit the floor and watched my little dog laboriously drag it—an object too large for his mouth—to where I could reach it. I realized first-hand the importance of service dogs to people with more permanent disabilities.

As my leg healed and I walked somewhere with a walker and eventually crutches, Dandi carefully kept out of my way as he had been trained. Once I was more mobile and able to get out, I applied to churches to be their pastor. Dandi accompanied me on interviews.

One of the first interviews occurred in early spring when I still used crutches. Dandi walked at my side like the dutiful assistance dog that he is. At one particular church, the search committee apparently did not know about my surgery and the fact that I was just beginning to get around. I had directions to a door with a set of stairs. Dismayed, I looked for a more accessible entrance, but I did not see one. Never having fully mastered the crutches to ascend stairs, I struggled up with Dandi beside me. I thought he looked at me compassionately. When we were half way up the seemingly endless stairs, the door opened and a search committee member greeted me. Apparently surprised by the somewhat disabled applicant, she looked down at Dandi with his service dog vest.

"Goodness!" she said incredulously. "Is he really a help to you?"

Once inside I explained Dandi's role as a service dog for ministry, and we all had a chuckle over the woman's apparent assumption that he somehow helped with my disability. They applauded my use of a service dog for ministry and understood how he could break the ice with people as well as help comfort the sick. I enjoyed the interview and committee members, hoping the church would call me, but it was not to be.

At another interview some weeks later, I noticed that search committee members eyed Dandi suspiciously.

"But what does that dog actually *do*?" asked one woman whom I had decided was not a dog lover. I explained his role as I had on the previous interview. He brought comfort and put people at ease. And sometimes he brought humor to situations.

"But what does it do when you are preaching?" the same woman persisted. I made a mental note of her use of it when referring to my beloved companion. No points for her in my book.

"He stays up near the pulpit with me," I explained with a smile, adding my well-used line. "And he is the only one encouraged to sleep through my sermons." Humor was lost on that critic. I certainly did not expect everyone to like or even appreciate dogs, but I decided that church was low on my list.

Eventually, my work on a committee brought me to the church that called me. I served on the executive committee for the Franklin Association of the United Church of Christ and had attended meetings for a year or so. The committee keeps communication open among the association's churches and among other committees charged with church business as well as planning annual meetings.

Serving on a committee is a wonderful way to learn what is going on in the area and of discovering churches searching for pastors. I enjoyed my tenure and Dandi slept peacefully at my side.

During one meeting, I learned that the pastor in Whately had left and the church needed someone to supply, that is guest preach while they looked for another minister. A committee member asked if I would be interested. Although I wanted a church of my own, I agreed to preach for the month of October.

The first Sunday in October, Dandi and I took the pulpit of the First Congregational Church of Whately in the large and bright sanctuary in the heart of the town. Many people have not heard of Whately. Some GPSes do not recognize the town or assume that the traveler wants to go instead to South Deerfield, the next town over.

Whately is a lovely town nestled between historical Old Deerfield and Sunderland, Hatfield, and Williamsburg. Its historic Whately Inn, an excellent restaurant, draws from miles around.

In the people of Whately, Dandi and I found rare and precious gems. They greeted us with friendly enthusiasm and accepted Dandi as service dog for ministry. He was not the first dog to grace the pulpit of the church. Lynks and his human partner, Ginny Evans, had been there as pastor and service dog some years before.

October went by quickly, and when the chair of Whately deacons asked if I would consider a call to be their pastor I could not say yes quickly enough. Although UCC churches are governed by the congregation and are relatively autonomous, there is a wider procedure to call a minister. Since church members and I knew that my path had not been in keeping with that procedure, we appealed for guidance to the conference minister who oversaw the Franklin association. We agreed that I would be called as temporary minister to Whately for the next year. If, at the end of a year, we concurred that we were a good match as minister and congregation, the church would invite me to stay, and I could seek ordination as a called pastor.

As the year progressed, I understood that I had been guided to the Whately church. From time to time, I spoke of the death of my son and how I had healed with the help of family, friends, psychotherapy, the ministry, and Dandi. One by one, congregants told me of their own losses of a child in youth or early adulthood. I remembered the question at my ecclesiastical council: "How will your son's death inform your ministry?"

And now I knew. What comfort the commonality of our experiences could have for many of my parishioners.

Sharing the Hope

Soon after I had completed my training with Dandi, Sheila, the NEADS director, asked if I would consider being on the board of directors. She thought I could fill the open slot for a client representative, and she also believed the board could use the expertise I had to offer as a psychiatric social worker. I had been a psychotherapist for many years. NEADS works with disabled people and resulting emotional responses, and Sheila felt the board would value my perspective. At the next election, I became a board member.

The NEADS board that I joined as a new service dog owner was the most caring group of people I had encountered in a professional setting.

By involving myself with the board, I learned about programs that trained Dandi and also had a first-hand, comprehensive view of work accomplished by NEADS.

Before a board meeting one evening, Sheila took me aside. " You have worked with PTSD, right?" Sheila began. She knew that my psychotherapeutic practice catered to those who had suffered childhood trauma often resulting in post-traumatic stress or PTSD. I told her about my doctoral dissertation endorsing development of a self-help book for PTSD victims.

Sheila explained that many veterans with service dogs have PTSD. In some cases, the symptoms troubled them more than their physical disabilities. "Could you help us develop a program to train service dogs to help veterans cope with PTSD?" Sheila asked.

Her request stunned me, but I felt eager to comply. I felt new to having a service dog, but I was familiar with PTSD and its treatment. I pondered over whether childhood trauma sufferers demonstrate different symptoms from veterans returning from combat.

I wondered if I were up to the task Sheila had enlisted me for. She spoke to other board members about our plans, and they replied enthusiastically. Their enthusiasm instilled deeper doubts in me. Could I do it? Could I plan such a program?

As I drove home from the meeting that evening along narrow dark roads through the woods, I asked myself again and again if I was up to the challenge. Sheila thought I could do it. I had expertise in PTSD. Why was I so nervous?

So consumed was I by my concerns that I could have hit the shape looming ahead, but somehow I braked for the animal in the middle of the road. Perhaps I saw it because of its large size and light color against the darkened asphalt. A dog, I thought, wondering why the thing did not move. But as it calmly stared at me and apparently confident at its right to be there, I realized it was not a dog. I quickly concluded that it must be a coyote. Coyotes are plentiful in the woods of central Massachusetts. I had seen them many times and heard them on many evenings as they congregated in the fields behind my house and howled.

But this creature did not have the tall, pointed ears, high-rumped stance, or pointed nose of a coyote. As I sat in my car, stopped and transfixed by the creature before me, I recognized the smaller rounded ears and broader snout. Deep yellow eyes stared back at me with a silent message as I recognized the wolf in my path. Wolves are rarely seen, and I marveled not only that the animal blocked my path so calmly on the deserted road but that he gazed at me apparently devoid of fear. He stood beautiful and majestic.

And then I thought of Jamie with his love of the noble creatures.

The wolf and I stared at each other, each of us transfixed, perhaps, by the same message from beyond this realm. I am not sure how long we observed each other, but it seemed like a long while. And then, the beautiful creature turned and walked very slowly into the woods beside the road. Before disappearing into the underbrush, the wolf stopped briefly and glanced back at me as if in a final goodbye.

For a moment I sat, fortunate, I suppose, that no other car had come around the bend and collided with me, stopped as I was in the middle of the road. All tension of indecision evaporated. I knew I would do as Sheila asked. I was meant to do it. The wolf felt like a messenger—from Jamie perhaps—that I was in the right place at the right time and the right person to design a program to help veterans like my son.

Over the next few weeks, I read everything I could find on combat-related PTSD as experienced by those returning from Iraq and Afghanistan. I reviewed, too, what I already knew about PTSD— and its diagnosis based on three categories of symptoms. I already knew that PTSD symptoms fall into three categories: re-experiencing, avoidance or numbing, and arousal. When someone with PTSD re-experiences the traumatic events that overwhelmed the psyche so much as to cause the condition, it may take the form of flashbacks, nightmares, or panic attacks when it feels like the event recurs. Or PTSD may manifest as intense physical reactions as the individual may have had when the traumatic experience took place. I had seen clients in my therapy office with racing heart beat, tense muscles, rapid breathing, and even nausea. They often felt plagued by intrusive memories as if they could never escape them.

The natural response to such horrendous memories is to want to avoid them by isolating oneself and losing interest in all activities because of potential reminders of the trauma experience. People with PTSD often do not want to talk about the trauma and adopt a sense of numbness because feelings have become frightening. I had talked with service members who avoided crowds because life in war-torn countries always seemed to be in crowds, and crowds represent danger. They had a difficult time readjusting to groups of people once discharged because of persistent memory of the sense of danger that they had felt. They often could not trust others. Who knew who was an enemy and who was not?

Despite attempts to avoid memories of traumatic events, survivors of PTSD may themselves exist in a constant state of arousal, always on guard for danger. Such a state makes it difficult to sleep, can make one irritable or angry, causes one to be jumpy and startle easily, and can lead to inability to concentrate on a task at hand.

As I reviewed symptoms by comparing signs of combat-related PTSD with signs of childhood trauma, fleeting bits of conversation flashed through my mind.

"I used to think that the world was an okay place," echoed my son Jamie's words from a distant night, "but it can be a pretty dangerous place."

"You can't really trust anyone!"

"Sometimes I see pictures in my head. They frighten me and I wish they would just go away!"

I thought of evenings when Jamie and I talked well into the night—of the one night when, his body tense, unyielding, a sheen of perspiration across his brow, he told me of the horrors he had experienced in Bosnia. There were the nights when Jamie's wandering throughout the house awakened me as, haunted by demons I could not fathom, he could not sleep. I remember how he refused to attend a Christmas celebration of his father's large family, an event he would have once thoroughly enjoyed.

"There are just too many people," he told me, "And I don't feel so great. I'm just going back to bed."

"But Jamie," I said, "It is only noon. You won't sleep tonight if you sleep all day."

"What's the point, Mom?" he had responded. "I don't sleep at night no matter what I do."

The memories drifted through my consciousness accompanied by a profound guilt. I was a therapist. I had worked with post-traumatic stress for years, and yet I had not admitted to myself that my son exhibited all the symptoms and needed help.

The realization made me determined to help with the program for veterans with PTSD and let Sheila know I would develop it. Despite later media coverage about using service dogs to help address PTSD, in 2007 it was new. I had no real guidelines nor prototype for how to develop such a program. Sheila suggested I be in touch with Kathy Foreman, the NEADS client coordinator whose excellent selections of prospects for placement with a dog contribute greatly to the agency's success.

Kathy assisted in developing a program to address PTSD. She knew the needs of the veterans who already had service dogs. She understood the need for designing a program to address PTSD. Ready for the challenge, I revised the service dog application with PTSD in mind and developed other tools to assess the needs of veterans with PTSD and our ability to help them.

I am also a certified graphologist, able to assess personality characteristics present in handwriting. I thought it would be interesting if we tracked changes in our veterans' handwriting once they worked with their dogs. Thus, graphology became another measurement tool, although we did not widely publicize it because of skepticism some people have about handwriting analysis. We found substantial differences in writings of veterans from the point of application to after they had their dogs. We saw that handwriting analysis was a valuable tool.

Kathy and I began working with two talented dog trainers, Brian Jennings, who had trained my dog, and Erin Wiley, a trainer mentored by Brian, to develop criteria for training dogs for veterans with PTSD. We brainstormed about the type of dog that veterans would need. Given that many veterans have difficulty with loud noises and often feel out of control, their dogs must be calm and take little notice of noises or unexpected events. Veterans could therefore rely upon their dogs as barometers of actual rather than perceived danger.

Dogs must also be consistent and reliable so that wary veterans can depend upon their dogs to remain in control when veterans themselves felt out of control. For the most part, then, we could not use shelter dogs. When dogs end up in shelters, they have often themselves been wounded—not physically, perhaps, but past experiences may have negatively impacted their temperament. A wounded dog lacks confidence and often responds either by falling apart or displaying aggression. We acknowledged that dogs that we used must be the cream of the canine crop, confident but amenable to bonding with their veterans and gaining their trust.

We knew the kinds of dogs we wanted for the program but still had to determine how veterans would use them. I envisioned dogs helping their veterans by serving as a bridge between them and their environment. Dogs would help reintegrate veterans into the larger society as the men and women gained trust and confidence in their own abilities to interact with others. Taking each symptom of PTSD and guiding veterans in how to use their dogs to cope, I wrote a helpful manual. We decided we would teach veterans skills through a variety of techniques I would develop.

I wondered what Jamie would have thought of such a program. Would such a program have changed the course of his life and prevented his untimely death?

Mirror Image

As we began to interview and place dogs with veterans, we were all touched in many ways. I interviewed applicants about their post-traumatic stress and many of them shared the events that led to their trauma. Not unlike my son's experience, young men left home, often right out of high school, to suddenly face events far out of their frames of reference. As they told me of their experiences, I felt their confusion and their pain. They experienced anguish at cruel scenarios playing out before their eyes—the deaths of friends, the injustices of combat. Many had been victims of blasts of IEDs or homemade mini bombs that often left them with traumatic brain injury, TBI. More than one veteran admitted that he had thought of taking his own life and that some of his former comrades had done just that.

They spoke of how they began to feel out of sync with the worlds they had once known—the girlfriends and wives who could not understand the changes they saw and the people who wanted the gory details of what they had experienced. How many veterans returned from combat plagued not only by the symptoms of PTSD but also by the alienation they feel from loved ones who expect them to be the same person who donned a uniform and marched off to war. As I interviewed our applicants, I was reminded of Jamie's words.

"My friends just don't get it, Mom. It's not their fault, but they've been at college or working and have no idea of the things I've seen. It's like we can't really communicate on the same level."

The veterans I interviewed had dealt with their feelings of alienation in different ways. Some had withdrawn, unable to face a world that could not understand what they had seen or experienced. Others struck out in anger, driving away those they loved, disregarding the law, and sometimes getting arrested. Some had turned to alcohol or drugs in the hope of dulling the pain. But all those we interviewed had emerged to some degree—at least to understand that they must reinvent themselves and find ways to go on. The men we saw were emerging success stories, those who had pulled themselves from the depths of despair—who realized they needed help and perhaps that help could be found in part through partnering with a service dog.

As I watched veteran after veteran and heard their stories unfold, I wondered where they had found the strength to go on— how they had recognized that the precious value of life. What had helped them to move on when my son could not?

Perhaps the strength of spirit I saw in those men pushed me to seek answers—to discover what was different in Jamie's life. Was he not as well loved as many of the veterans? Did he not realize that life is too filled with promise to throw it away? Through working with veterans, my own healing truly began. I knew I had to face some of the difficult considerations that I had not been able to face before.

With resolution, I pored over the police report and Jamie's autopsy. Immediately following his death, in denial that my spirited son could have killed himself, I searched for other explanations. Perhaps someone else had shot him. Could he have been inadvertently shot by the police at the scene? And yet, as I read the autopsy it became clear to me that the bullet that killed my son had been fired in such a way that only he could have done it. That realization was inordinately painful.

I tried to piece together what might have led to the events of the night and early morning that would culminate in his death.

I thought again of the months after he returned home from the military. Yes, he was different, tortured perhaps, not entirely knowing who he was or where he was going.

"I feel like a misfit," he had said when he came home from college one weekend. "I don't feel like being with my old friends anymore. They have no idea what I've seen and can't understand how I feel. They seem like kids to me, and I feel so old."

Another thought crept into my consciousness—one I had tried desperately to forget. But there it was, forcing its way into my reality, a diabolical reminder of my own guilt.

It was early December. Jamie was still at college, and Gwen was living with us. Clearly they were no longer a couple. I knew by then that when the semester ended, Jamie would not return to college. Given his own disquiet and the pressure the girl placed on him to come home to be with her, I suspected that he had not done well. I wondered what would happen when Jamie came home for good—all under the same roof but like individual planets operating each in our own solar orbits—me busy with my work as a pastor, Jamie and Gwen together but no longer together, Jim with his work.

One afternoon that December, Gwen came to me looking defiant. We expected Jamie home that evening for a brief respite before his final exams began.

"I'm pregnant," she announced without preamble. I wasn't sure I heard her correctly. I no longer thought of Jamie and Gwen as a couple. That was in the past—something spent and over. Was there someone else? No, she seemed never to stay anywhere else. She had made no other friends despite our efforts to help her do so.

"It's Jamie's," she pronounced as if reading my thoughts. I had no illusions that they had not been intimate. As I mentally counted back, I realized the pregnancy probably began soon after she arrived in October. My first thought was that she would destroy my son's life. I am not proud of that initial reaction, but I had decided she was a tortured soul.

"We could get married," she continued and my fears grew. I knew that Jamie no longer loved her. He had already shared with me that no matter how much he had wanted to save her from herself, he could not accomplish the task. Although I suspected he would stand by her, I doubted he would be happy married to her. I envisioned their lives as a constant battle if what I had seen in recent months indicated anything.

I do not remember my response to Gwen's pronouncement if I gave one at all. Did she expect me to be overjoyed as a potential grandmother? I could not think about that. Did she envision my congratulatory hugs? I had seen too many young people marry for the wrong reasons, and I felt the pregnancy may have been her way to induce my compassionate son to marry her. Jamie would be home soon, and she would tell him, I concluded. I wondered what his response would be.

That evening blurs in my mind. I do remember her angry taunt, "Well, I will just get an abortion then!"

I was not privy to my son's response when Gwen gave him her news. He, too, probably realized that life would change forever if the child came into the world—that he or she might be held hostage in the war between his parents. He left the house right after she told him and did not return until after I was in bed. Over the next few days, Jamie drew into himself and I could not reach him. My loving son who adored children and could not wait to have his own was clearly fighting some inner battle that excluded me. He was in the midst of exams and returned to college to finish them. I wondered if he could possibly concentrate.

A picture flashes through my mind—a cold mid-December day, sitting in the waiting room of an abortion clinic with Gwen beside me. I felt cold—inside and out. By his choice or hers, I had no idea, but Jamie had not accompanied the girl. Although I expected her tears, she had none but chatted calmly. She said it would be her third abortion. I don't remember how I reacted, so caught up was I in my own pain. I could not think of what would soon happen as destroying life. I could only hold on to being Mama Bear, convinced that somehow the abortion would save my son's life. The irony of it all. As I look back, I wonder how much that day and my collusion with Gwen contributed to his death. Would a baby have caused him to choose to live? I cannot think about it; the pain is too overwhelming.

As I reflect on it, the abortion merges with other events to illuminate Jamie's mindset just before his death. How many of the veterans with whom I worked had relationship issues? How many were disappointed by the cards life dealt them and estranged from those who once meant much to them?

I wondered, too, if Jamie's disillusionment with Gwen whom he once thought he loved, was combined with the loss of the child they could have had. Did that and his troubled school performance lead to his elation when initial orders to Iraq had come through? He knew how to be a soldier; he would not have had to start something new but instead continue a way of life he understood. His waiting and hoping for a deployment date only to have it postponed again and again and again must have added to his anxiety and intensified his depression. Had the cancellation of those orders, being told that he was not needed in Iraq after all, pushed him toward the events of that May morning?

He had tried to pick up the pieces. After he learned he would not be deployed, he had found a job working with disturbed kids. But was returning to normalcy after all the emotional assaults he had experienced just not possible for him? Other men and women had made the transition. Other soldiers had returned home and found a way to fit back into civilian lives despite PTSD. What was so different about my son?

Through the Glass Darkly

We will never know what actually happened in the wee hours of the morning of May 18, 2003. Why did my beloved son—a young man who grew up with all indications that he was gentle, caring and far from violent—go to a home with a stolen weapon, enter into some kind of altercation with the people there, and ultimately take his own life? As I wrote this memoir, I thought of the speculations that have emerged in the sixteen years since all of this happened.

When the media first covered the horrific events of that day—accounts that I would not hear nor read until much later—one of Jamie's friends reported to me that the TV account implied that there were two other young people there. If so, why were they never mentioned later? One newspaper account mentioned that Gwen was staying at the house with another friend. What happened to her?

Gwen told the media that she believed Jamie had come to kill her. And yet, when he and I talked two nights before the events, his feelings sounded anything but hostile toward her. In fact, he felt aggrieved because he was afraid that she had become involved with drugs and headed down a path he feared. And if his intent was to kill her, how had Jamie, an expert marksman, not accomplished that goal? He could easily have surprised the girl and her boyfriend and killed them both. But he didn't. The boyfriend was injured slightly, but the location of the wound—an ear—was more likely from a struggle than from an outright aimed shot or, on the other hand, may have been the work of the truly expert marksman. Jamie's autopsy indicated that there were neither drugs nor alcohol in his system. If he had a clear head and no moral reservation, killing the two unsuspecting young people would have been logistically easy.

I remembered pictures I had seen of Jamie with his assault weapon and was painfully aware that my son had been trained by the Army not only to shoot but to kill. He was prepared for combat, for taking down an enemy with little thought. Gwen and her friend were not trained as soldiers, thus giving Jamie a decided advantage if his goal had been to kill them.

Despite being schooled in marksmanship by the military, Jamie had spent his first eighteen years in a home with no guns. Violence was not the norm. He had learned to handle disputes not by power-over tactics but rather by discussion and negotiation. Jamie was by nature the rescuer, not someone to bring harm to others.

I remember Jamie's pride when he became an expert marksman in the Army, pride perhaps based on being able to learn a required skill and do it well. I also think of his disillusionment when he realized that he had been taught to kill people, not just aim at paper targets. Could four years of military training have so totally wiped out eighteen years of moral teachings that he would be capable of the premeditation to kill? Somehow, I found it hard to imagine.

Recent literature about veterans describes a phenomenon called moral injury. Coined by psychiatrist Jonathan Shay, the term moral injury refers to the emotional—or even spiritual impact on an individual who is exposed to or participates in events or acts that violate the moral code or one's understanding of what is right that has been instilled.

The individual has either been compelled to participate in acts of transgression, has failed to prevent what he feels is morally wrong, or has had to witness contradictions to his moral code. Further, according to understanding of the phenomenon of moral injury, the soldier feels betrayed by someone who holds legitimate authority.

While PTSD relates to external experience, moral injury occurs internally. PTSD creates fear of a variety of stimuli in an individual with resulting symptoms of hyper arousal and avoidance of anything that reminds the individual of the traumas of war or other shocking experiences. Moral injury—which may or may not exist along with PTSD—leads to difficulty of individuals in fully trusting others or even themselves. Many men and women stationed in war-torn countries see or participate in acts against the moral code instilled in them during their early years. Even more complex, military training presents a new code. "Thou shalt not kill," taught in early religious or ethical training, gets set aside in favor of the language of war—kill or be killed for a just cause.

Many seventeen-, eighteen-, or nineteen-year-olds raise their hands to swear acceptance of the revised moral code. Research tells us that the moral brain has not fully developed during the teen years, so it stands to reason that exposure to moral dilemmas presents difficulty for young soldiers. Some young people accept the new moral code of military training as their new normal, while others—particularly those have experienced exposure to strong moral values that emphasize the sanctity of all life—may find themselves confused, distressed, and plagued by moral injury.

Some young trainees may see betrayal by those in authority who expect them to abandon previously held values in order to espouse the emphases of military training. For example, despite a young soldier's love of children, superiors admonish that soldier to drive through without comment when a group of civilians, even one including children, block the path of the soldier's tank. The military rationale asserts that the tank driver has no way of knowing if the civilians intend to ambush the military company or merely to go about their own lives. If the group plans to ambush, the military company risks death if the driver should hesitate. So, the military admonishes soldiers not to stop.

Theories of moral injury assert that military rationales that challenge an individual's personal moral code can result in shame, guilt, regret, and a deep sense of loss.

As I learned more and more about moral injury, I thought of Jamie—the once sensitive young man who saved the lost and injured, whether animals or people—who loved children and often lent a hand in kindness. I have no doubt that Jamie battled with moral injury as he tried to make sense of what he saw in war-torn Bosnia. Even as he befriended children, he witnessed injustices done to them that he could not prevent. He grieved for the young women rape victims of ethnic cleansing and marveled at the strength of those who survived. He also likely found it difficult to understand how some of his fellow soldiers seemed not to have the same respect for human life and dignity that he did.

I think again and again about his late-night phone call to me from boot camp when he tearfully recounted that he realized the human-shaped targets he had hit successfully at the shooting range could soon be replaced by flesh and blood men and woman.

Experts refer to the soul damage of moral injury that leaves the one who experiences it confused, guilt-ridden, and searching for a way to recalibrate the personal moral compass. Such psychiatric distress can prompt a veteran to self-harm or, paradoxically, adopt aggression as a method of solving personal problems. Moral injury often goes hand-in-hand with PTSD further complicating the picture.

Could moral outrage at injustices and violence also create someone who goes overboard to protect others from perceived harm? I have wondered, too, if Jamie's objective was to protect the girl from something, not harm her. That plan would certainly have been in keeping with how he spoke of her in our last talk together. He told me he felt responsible for bringing Gwen so far from her home and, even though they were not meant to be together, he wanted to be sure that she had a good life. Would he then have attempted to kill her or instead have wanted to protect her from whatever he perceived as the threat to her wellbeing? The fact that Gwen herself told me she had left the room when Jamie came in supports my thought. If his desire was to kill her, would he not have followed her?

In the days right after Jamie's death, I could not believe that he had taken his own life. I remember when Jamie seemed quite discouraged during one of our mother-son talks. It may have been when his orders to Iraq were finally canceled. He had been eager to return to active duty and here he was—having dropped out of college and broken up with Gwen. He confessed that he felt without a purpose for his life. My therapist training kicked in and, concerned about his discouragement, I found myself screening him for suicidal thoughts.

"Have you thought of taking your own life?" I finally asked him with a bluntness that seemed to surprise him.

"Oh, Mom," he began, looking at me with sincere intensity. "I could never do that to you."

As I tried to make sense of his death and yearning to find an explanation other than suicide, I pored over the death certificate. But there it was in bold jarring print. Suicide. Jamie had done the one thing he knew would have a devastating impact on me. Why? I searched for answers with the intensity of one who must understand in order to find wholeness.

I remembered the last note Jamie left me. I never saw it as a suicide note, because he left it the day before he died. But perhaps it was.

Concerned about the outcome of the hearing for the restraining order Gwen had taken out against him, he left me that note. I played it over in my mind once again.

Dear Mom,

The wolf cannot be caged. Whatever happens, I will always love you.

Child of your heart,

Jamie

After he died, I thought the note was strange, but I did not see it as a final goodbye. That fulfilling talk Jamie and I had that night convinced me he had found a direction for his life. He said he loved his new job in the residential treatment center. After several days of work, he had decided he would enjoy working with emotionally disturbed teens. He had completed an application to the local community college and planned to work and go to classes part time toward getting a degree. He seemed back on track, and when we both went to bed after our late night talk two evenings before his death, I felt confident that my son had found himself. What happened from that night until the next, when everything would take such a drastic turn?

I often wonder if the answers lie in some interaction between him and Gwen. After his death, the police never returned his cell phone. Had he received a call that would shed light on how events had evolved? My attempt to piece things together prompted my call to the state trooper asking that Jamie's belongings be returned to me. His characteristic accusatory tone as he questioned me about what belongings I thought they had made me feel that I was somehow complicit. When I got off the phone, I felt shaken and that my request for Jamie's belongings had not been acknowledged nor honored. We never got them back. The interchange was so unpleasant that I did not pursue it again.

I was left to wonder and speculate. What took Jamie to the home of Gwen's new boyfriend? How did he even know where to go? And how did his mindset change from a young man who had put disillusionment over lost love behind him and found new purpose to someone who could steal a gun, break into a house, and be described as a potential killer before taking his own life?

As I worked with other young men with PTSD and assisted them in obtaining service dogs, I heard stories that helped put Jamie's into some perspective. Feeling betrayed by life and by their loved ones, some veterans found outlets both self-destructive and dangerous to others. Many returning veterans have scrapes with the law. Trained to see guns as not only their "battle buddies" but necessary for protection, some veterans insisted upon having a gun by their sides. They described the volatility of their emotions that could change from moment to moment. Taught by the military to be what one veteran described as "killing machines," they found it difficult to readjust to civilian life.

I knew in retrospect that his PTSD plagued Jamie. I couldn't help but notice his sleepless nights prowling around the house like a caged animal, his intense startle reflex when he was touched unexpectedly or when there was a loud noise, or the times when his anger bubbled so dangerously close to the surface and his debilitating depression at times were all classic symptoms. As a therapist, I should have bundled him off to a colleague skilled in PTSD, but I was so caught up in the drama of our lives at the time that I may not have fully recognized the syndrome. I am not sure if he would have gone if I had I tried to encourage him to go.

Jamie had been brought up in the home of a psychotherapist, me, and had actually gone for some brief counseling as a teen when our divorce was difficult for him to handle. But he also trained in the military, and I knew that the prevailing sentiment in the service was to avoid mental health professionals for fear one be considered weak or unfit. "It's a macho thing," one of the male veterans I counseled told me, but military women were also less likely to seek counseling than civilians.

Both military men and women are more likely to seek out a chaplain than a psychotherapist to discuss their problems and concerns. As the daughter of a military chaplain, I had witnessed the phenomenon, only to have it confirmed by the veterans with whom I worked.

As my son was wrestling with his PTSD demons, I was both training for the ministry and practicing as a psychotherapist. Why did I not fully recognize Jamie's PTSD? I know that my first reactions were as a mother who wanted to cuddle and soothe rather than those of a mental health professional who realized the implications of what I was seeing. But perhaps there was more to it than that.

During the year that Jamie, Gwen, and I were embroiled in our drama, I was also completing my clinical pastoral education at a local hospital. When I anticipated the training required of all seminary students, I was glad I had psychology training and assumed it would be helpful. But my supervisor had other ideas and constantly cautioned me to stop thinking like a psychologist and, instead, think like a minister. I once visited a patient who was extremely depressed, and my therapist antennae urged me to screen him for suicide. I did so. When I reported what I had done to my supervisor, she told me it was not my role. I found the admonition difficult to accept. Nonetheless, the de-emphasis of my psychology training may well have spilled over into what I saw happening at home.

Had I seen with different eyes, would I have realized how trapped my son felt? Jamie told me once during his post military time that he could never go to a zoo again. He could never again watch caged animals pacing with purposeless intensity, going nowhere, feeling helpless.

"That's how I feel sometimes," he told me "It's like I will never get out of this rut of feeling vulnerable and angry and on guard while at the same time having no control over feeling that way."

Was it the PTSD that had somehow influenced his last night and brought him to the disastrous conclusion? What part of his military training kicked in that caused him to break into a home? I have seen the movie *American Sniper* and similar depictions of the search and destroy missions for which the military is trained. I can only imagine the adrenaline that must kick in as, intent upon rooting out an enemy, one forces one's way into a domicile. How much of that training follows a soldier once he is back in civilian life? Did Jamie see that he had a mission to accomplish? Was it search and destroy as the girl assumed, or was it a rescue mission by Jamie who throughout his life had been the rescuer?

If Gwen was correct, that my son's intent was to harm her or her latest lover, what stopped him from doing it? Chance? Did they somehow elude his assault? Or was there a moment when the lessons of his childhood prevailed? Had he wrestled with his military training and his own moral code to do no wrong that stopped him at the crucial moment before he killed the girl and her companion?

Or, if his intent was to rescue the girl from some perceived evil, did he discover that Gwen had herself chosen to be in that house and, thus, did not require or want Jamie's help?

I envision his thoughts as a kaleidoscope of partially formed instincts, memories, and values vying with each other to direct his actions. How confused and pained he must have been in those last moments.

Trying to understand his mindset, I imagined myself in my son's place. I could empathize with all he had gone through in the past months. His relationship with Gwen had soured and grew increasingly stressful. Not only disillusioned by what could have been between them, he also likely grieved for the child that might have been.

Reintegration into civilian life after the military did not occur easily for that young soldier. As with so many others at the time, the army provided no preparation for returning to civilian life after his military service. Because of his reserve status, perhaps the army deemed no need for help with a transition back to civilian life. That said, surely his previous life in a war-torn country fraught with perils and dangers contrasted greatly to the day-to-day in the small town where Jamie returned to live with his mother, stepfather, and former girlfriend. Deprived of camaraderie with his brothers in arms, he had no one who shared his experiences and, therefore, understood them. Like fellow veterans and as a remnant of the stress of military duty, Jamie remained alert for any potential threat.

Culture shock owed not only to the difference of living in a small town. Jamie no longer had the rigorous routine and rigid expectations of military life. Out of the military, he had no imposed schedule. After four years of a highly organized life, he was at a loss about how to organize his time. He must have wondered about his identify. No longer an active soldier, apparently not needed for deployment, no longer a college student, unable to find a full-time job with his future uncertain, experiencing the aftermath of a difficult relationship, Jamie no doubt felt lost and unable to control his own life. The roller coaster of promised deployments and cancellations must have added to his feelings that he could not control much.

My thoughts circled me once again back to my haunted question of why Jamie took his own life. Had his jumbled thoughts overwhelmed him? Or, with clarity, was he the caged wolf who saw no other relief than to take his own life? Had his nagging symptoms and the fear of being caged either figuratively or literally as a result of the behavior caused him to end his life? He would not have been the first soldier with PTSD to do so. Did he recognize what he had done by committing the crimes of theft, breaking and entering, and attempted assault and, thus, realize that the result would be prosecution and possibly incarceration—being literally caged?

"I could not do that to you, Mom," Jamie had said of committing suicide, but would he see the disgrace of what he had done and the result as more hurtful to me and the rest of his family? I cannot fathom seeing my son behind bars and knowing what it would do to his soul: the wolf who could not be caged. And I thought of the words he had read me long ago.

I remembered Jamie explaining how people misunderstand wolves, often depicted in fairy and folk tales and even nonfiction accounts as bloodthirsty and even evil. Yet, in reality, intelligent, friendly, loyal wolves devote themselves to their families. At the same time, meant to be free, wolves embody the spirit of the wild.

Perhaps, I thought as I reread the passage Jamie had shown me, Jamie's spirit could not even be confined to this earth, this lifetime. I remember him once saying to me when he was a very young teen, "Mom, I am not of this earth." I remember thinking that it's a strange thing for a child or teen to say. Now I wonder if a part of him—even at such a young age—had a prophetic knowledge of how it would end.

What happened that last night and early morning of my son's life on this earth?

In the end there is only one conclusion we can come to. No one knows what really happened. Even those reportedly present—the girl and another young man—have witness statements colored by their own experience and interpretation. They, too, can speculate, but neither of them can know what motivated Jamie nor his intent.

The only entirely accurate conclusion: we will never fully know.

But I can always hold tightly to my memories as a mother and what I knew of the child of my heart.

Prisms

"I'm glad that you are healing from your PTSD," my therapist colleague commented as we had lunch together a few years ago. We had been discussing the fact that I was writing a memoir about Jamie's death and how his death led me to work with combat veterans and service dogs. "PTSD? I didn't have PTSD. You are thinking of Jamie," I returned.

"Really?" she shot back. "What would you call extreme depression, feelings of hopelessness, the inability to find pleasure in life, flashbacks, anxiety, nightmares—all related to traumatic events? After all, you not only lost your son in a violent, traumatic way that caused people to talk about the events for months to come, but you lived with him in the throes of his own PTSD and his chaotic relationship for months. Not to mention losing a major emotional support—your mom—very soon after. Ever heard of secondary PTSD?"

She wasn't telling me anything I didn't know about survivors' PTSD and even secondary PTSD. I have worked with enough family members of veterans with PTSD to know that secondary PTSD is a real phenomenon. In fact, I had written a manual for NEADS explaining to partners of NEADS veterans that the months and years of living with someone with PTSD takes its toll on those who love them. Symptoms of those living with someone experiencing PTSD often mirror those of the veteran and are known as secondary PTSD or vicarious traumatization. Even therapists who work with traumatized patients may exhibit vicarious traumatization after a while.

I thought of the spouses I had counseled who could not understand why they began to exhibit symptoms of anxiety, depression, and hopelessness.

"I should be there for my husband!" one wife sobbed. "And now I feel like I am developing the same problems he has been battling. What's wrong with me?"

You are human, I thought and counseled as I would so many times, and you have been living with someone you love who is in incredible emotional pain. Sometimes in the intensity of our empathy and exposure to that pain, we take it on ourselves.

I also realized through my work with family members whose veterans died by suicide that many family members experienced their own battles with PTSD.

"As I thought of how my son died—by his own hand-," one mother began as I sat with her in an effort to help her process her son's death. My own heart ached as she went on.

"I could just imagine his last hours. How much pain he must have been in to choose to end his life rather than fighting through it. It must have seemed so hopeless if he would take that step." Such pain does something to those who love in the way that mother did. Finding her son dead impacted her so deeply that she, too, soon revealed symptoms that we identify as PTSD.

As I thought about my colleague's words, spoken as we sat alone together in a quiet restaurant, I realized after the fact that I, too, had experienced secondary PTSD. But even though I had recognized secondary PTSD in other survivors of those who had taken their own lives after experiencing combat-related PTSD, I had not immediately identified it in myself. Someone else—not me.

And yet, in a moment of clarity, I knew that she was correct.

"I guess I never thought about it that way," I told my friend. And then as an afterthought, "Just as I did not recognized the full extent of Jamie's PTSD," I added quietly.

"You can't keep beating yourself up about that," admonished my colleague. "You're not the only one who wasn't acknowledging military PTSD then. It's been around forever, but until recently, it was the elephant in the room that no one wanted to name. Furthermore, it's tougher when it is your own child."

In the days before proper identification of PTSD, I remembered hearing the insensitive description "shell-shocked" to describe the condition of a veteran reluctant to go into combat or diving into a corner at the sound of a loud noise. I felt somehow soothed that my respected colleague gave me the permission to forgive myself. I thought I had forgiven myself by then, but her words provided even more validation. I have thought often in the last few years of that lunch with my wise friend. We often expect those left behind by veteran suicide—by any suicide, really—to grieve just like those faced with any death of a loved one. But suicide, war, and PTSD confront survivors with extra layers of pain to address. Perhaps we need to be gentle with them, just as I had to be with myself. Healing happens from the inside out, but the complexity of what happens for the survivor of a loved one's suicide means multiple additional layers of healing.

Recognizing fully my place among survivors as I battled with my own PTSD increases my ability to help others. Everyone's experience—everyone's pain—is unique, but by fully understanding your own pain, you may be more available to help others cope with their unique pain.

A Mother's Reflections

I have learned a great deal from writing this book. It has been cathartic, disturbing and at the same time comforting. Soul searching has also been humbling.

I pride myself on being a competent therapist and have worked with PTSD for many years. Yet, I did not comprehend the magnitude of the influence of PTSD on my son's life nor, in fact, that he suffered from it until I looked back on events leading to his death.

No doubt veterans I met through my work with service dogs while wearing my professional hat helped me piece things together. As I heard them speak of their experiences, I had to confront the likelihood that my son numbered among them and had experienced horrors like what they described. The experiences of what they had seen or even done in combat left them in confusion and emotional pain I recognize from my work: pain distorts the way people interpret reality. For some veterans, reality is that death seems preferable to dealing with the pain. Granted, everyone reacts differently to the horrific events of war, but there are enough similarities in human emotions to know that Jamie must have shared at least some of the feelings that the veterans in our program described.

No matter how I see these veterans and their experiences through the lens of a therapist, when it comes to the bare bones of the matter, Jamie was my son. My experience and response was first as his mother. When I heard veterans speak about their training and paint pictures of how they used that training and carried out their roles as soldiers, I came to recognize that my son had acted as a soldier.

I remember photos I found after his death depicting Jamie and his buddies with their guns in mock readiness, mugging for the camera. Was it their way of coping with how they would use the assault weapons if called upon? It was difficult for me to see my once gentle son embrace a military rifle knowing that he would probably have used it—and may have used it.

I also recognized as I listened to my veterans that there was no way that I could ever comprehend and therefore understand what they and my own son had experienced in war-torn countries.

Someone recently told me that she felt that war was like growing up in an abusive family. No one wants to speak about the details. It is too painful to recount experiences because to do so can bring them back in Technicolor. And what you did to survive the horrors is often too shame-provoking to admit to anyone else.

I can never know what my son experienced nor how those events and encounters etched themselves on his soul. We as parents find it painful when our children are hurt or subjected to trauma. From their first scratched knee, we ache for them and want to coddle and comfort. But some wounds are too deep, and because we lack understanding of them, they are too far out of our reach to soothe. If love was enough to ease whatever pain Jamie experienced or to prevent his suicide, he would be with us today, for we loved him deeply, and so did many others. But I have learned that love is not always enough.

I have also realized that I must forgive myself for not recognizing the depth of my son's pain and not being able to prevent his death. No matter how skilled I may or may not be as a therapist, love sometimes blinds us to what we might see wearing a professional hat.

I ache for the child of my heart and what he experienced as a soldier. That whole period occurred between his eighteenth and twenty-first years when many formerly sheltered children like my son are just getting their feet wet on a college campus or at their first real job. But my son experienced a world where killing is expected, death almost routine, and the dignity of the individual must often be sacrificed to get a job done. Jamie, a young man who had never experienced death among family or friends, found himself witnessing the digging up of mass graves to rebury the dead.

At his post, he lived through the constant threat of death from minefields, grim reminders of a country at war that made it impossible to explore the Bosnian countryside. How can such experiences not have an impact? And what of ever-present danger? Young men and women raised in insulated small towns as Jamie was may never have been acquainted with the fear of knowing that, at any moment, you may step on a mine, be shot at, or witness the killing or maiming of another. For soldiers, all are constant concerns.

When our children make the decision that their lives are too difficult to repair, we, their parents, are left incredulous as to why we could not have somehow prevented them from taking the life we gave them and nurtured with all our hopes and dreams for a future that will never be. Just as we did not know nor understand our children's pain, so can they never understand or know the depth of ours.

As I stand among others whose sons or daughters have died by their own hands as a result of their experiences in the military, I share with them the aloneness of being a parent whose child chose to end his or her life rather than face the incredible struggle to reintegrate into society after the impact of war. Granted, some veterans struggle through substance abuse, mental illness, or homelessness. But they persevere despite the struggle, and we have the opportunity to help them.

When a child is gone, we no longer have that opportunity. While parents who have lost their children in combat receive the sympathy of others and praise for their children's service and sacrifice, we parents of the lost through suicide fight the shame that separates us from those proud parents who paradoxically find honor in grief. When our children have taken their own lives, unable to endure the pain of reintegration, it is difficult to tell others what happened. In fact, it becomes so painful that we often hide the facts as I did for so long. Yet, when we seek to understand what our children experienced, their confusion and their pain, the wound dulls, if only slightly.

I hope that knowing our story will help parents and other loved ones still seeking the truth to unpack theirs.

A Blue Star mother gave me a great gift. She assured me that I am a Gold Star mother no matter how my son died. No one can dispute that my son served his country with pride and died as a result of wounds received during that service. She allowed me to lift my head a bit higher and seek to understand and accept why my son took the life his father and I had given him.

I hope, too, that others who have lost their children will take courage from this story. It is possible to make something worthy—something positive out of the shards of shattered glass you may feel are all that is left of your life.

The service dog program, now called the Trauma Assistance Dog program, would be the first of many assistance dog efforts to help veterans with PTSD. When I look at the young men—and later young women—whom this program and others like it would help, I give thanks that I had a part in reaching other veterans so that they would not take the route that Jamie did.

I am thankful for the healing I have gained through reaching out to others. Someone once told me that it is in tending another's wounds that ours are healed. Reflected from the veterans with whom I have worked, I found the perspective, strength and courage necessary to live a full life once again.

Through writing this book, I have learned—to quote the song—"that it is not what you take when you leave this world behind you, but what you leave behind when you go." My son left his caring legacy as he works through others and me to help veterans with PTSD in the hope of sparing them the painful choice that Jamie made.

And sometimes when I hear wolves howl in the distance at our summer cabin where Jamie's ashes rest—animals that run free as they were meant to do—I imagine that he speaks to me, urging me to keep on and live for him.

It is my gift from Jamie, the child of my heart.

Acknowledgments

There are so many people involved in writing and publishing a book, especially a memoir. As our lives become intertwined with others, we learn and grow and cannot help but be influenced. I have had some marvelous teachers along the path that brought me to writing *You Cannot Cage the Wolf*. I owe a great deal to my parents, James and Muriel Crosson, who taught me not only to love dogs and appreciate the bond with them but also how to be in touch with my own inner strength and resilience.

I have had the support of friends who nurtured and challenged me through the years. I am especially grateful to Kate Martin, Stephanie Flynn, Lois Buchiane, Bonnie Lee Nugent, Ellen Woodbury, and my wonderful Grapho Girls who keep up my spirits and keep me laughing.

I am thankful for friends and colleagues who read and reflected on the manuscript in its various stages, especially Carole Williams, Candace Anderson, Bonnie Lee Nugent, Beverly Prestwood-Taylor, Michelle DeLisio, Sharon Harmon, Charlie Tower, Virginia Allis, Peggy Prasinos, Bob Mayer, and Sheila O'Brien. Thanks to Sheila Lowe for our sharing about the loss of a child.

I am grateful to my family who walked this difficult road with me and were always there—Jim, Andrew, Chay, Becky, Ruby, and Charlie.

I have learned so much about myself through my work with service dogs and value those who have been an integral part of this process, especially Sheila O'Brien, Kathy Forman, Brian Jennings, Erin Wiley, Katy Ostroff, and the dedicated staff at NEADS.

And I am ever grateful to my beloved Dandi, who like others of his species knows all about unconditional love.

I also thank the members of the military families bereavement group, especially Patty and Paul and my co-facilitator Beverly Prestwood-Taylor, who have taught me that the healing continues even when you think you are done.

You Cannot Cage the Wolf would never have evolved had it not been for my talented editor and publisher, Marcia Gagliardi. From the first day when I stood in her office, my children's book about service dogs and veterans in hand, and uttered a timid, "I don't suppose you'd be interested in publishing my book," we established a bond that continues to be so important to me. Through the writing of *You Cannot Cage the Wolf,* Marcia listened, counseled, challenged, and edited until the product reflected my soul and hopefully will help other parents who have experienced the death of a military son or daughter. Thank you, Marcia for all you have given in time, guidance, counsel, and friendship.

And many thanks to those who helped with the publishing process, especially my copy editor Debra Ellis.

photo by Andrew Tower

Cynthia Crosson

About the Author

Cynthia Crosson, EdD, has written many widely read books about child welfare and trauma as well as two children's books that explain service dogs to children.

A licensed psychiatric social worker with a doctorate in counseling psychology, she specializes in trauma and PTSD. Her interest in trauma and her own life experiences took her to work with veterans and service dogs.

As she grew up, her family raised dogs. She became interested in the power of the human-dog connection. In 2005, she received an assistance dog for therapy and ministry from NEADS, an organization that places service dogs with individuals with disabilities. She later used her love of dogs and her knowledge of trauma to develop a program for NEADS to place service dogs with veterans suffering from combat related PTSD. The program has grown and became a model for other such programs across the country.

A minister in the United Church of Christ, the author serves a small church in Whately, Massachusetts. She lives with her husband and her aging assistance dog, Dandi, in Massachusetts where she works with service dogs and writes.

Colophon

Text for *You Cannot Cage the Wolf* is set in Adobe's FF Meta Serif designed by Botio Nikoltchev, Christian Schwartz, Erik Spiekermann, Kris Sowersby, and Ralph du Carrois. Intended for extended passages of text, FF Meta Serif uses conventional design techniques in a contemporary iteration for ease of reading.

Titles are set in Adobe's Ratio designed by Mark Caneso, founder of psType, which acts as the typographic side of pprwrk studio and offers contemporary designs both for retail and custom applications.

DATE DUE

DEC 1 6 2019		
JAN 0 6 2019		
FEB 2 6 2020		

THE LIBRARY STORE #47-0207

CPSIA information can be obtained
at www.ICGtesting.com
Printed in the USA
LVHW011547131119
637246LV00004B/55/P

9 781948 38017